ANNA Z/

# How did I get here?

A GUIDE TO LETTING GO OF YOUR PAST &
**LIVING IN ALIGNMENT WITH YOUR TRUE SELF**

*How did I get here?*

*A guide to letting go of your past and living in alignment with your true self*

First edition (2023)

Copyright ©Anna Zannides (2023)

All rights reserved.

No part of this publication may be reproduced, stored in a retrieval system, or transmitted in any form or by any means, without the prior written permission of the publisher.

Paperback ISBN: 978-1-7394589-0-4
eBook ISBN: 978-1-7394589-1-1

Published by Anna Zannides

www.annazannides.com

This book is dedicated to the most important people in my life, my children – Barris, Nicolas and Christos. I love you more than I can put into words.

And of course, to my three amazing granddaughters – Olivia, Sofia and Lila – I am privileged to have you in my life.

# Contents

| | |
|---|---|
| **Introduction** | 1 |
| **Part One: How Did I Get Here?** | 17 |
| Real Happiness | 25 |
| Forgetting Who You Are | 42 |
| Authenticity | 60 |
| **Part Two: This Is How You Got Here** | 69 |
| Love and Relationships | 72 |
| Gender Roles | 92 |
| Why Is Sex a Problem? | 123 |
| Being Schooled | 130 |
| Work and Money | 142 |
| **Part Three: What Will You Do with the Rest of Your Life?** | 155 |
| 1 – Freedom | 156 |
| 2 – Intuition | 161 |
| 3 – Awareness | 165 |
| 4 – Flow | 173 |
| 5 – Acceptance | 179 |
| 6 – Ageing | 189 |
| 7 – Spirituality | 196 |
| **Closing Note** | 199 |
| **Resources and Additional Support** | 203 |
| **About the Author** | 205 |

# Introduction

There are moments in life that shake us to the core and send us in a direction we never expected. It might be the abrupt ending of a relationship, a cancer diagnosis, the death of a loved one, a job loss or even a pandemic – all possible at any given moment and to which none of us are immune.

By the time I hit my fifties I thought I'd been through it all and life was going to be plain sailing from then on.

After years of hard work, teaching in secondary schools, I'd finally moved on to what I thought was my dream job as a national education adviser in a large academy trust. Not only did it take me out of the classroom, which I was finding increasingly stressful, it allowed me a degree of freedom because most of the time I'd be travelling around the country, visiting different schools.

A couple of years earlier, my husband and I had celebrated our thirty-year wedding anniversary, which was quite an achievement considering the many near misses we'd had throughout our marriage. Yet, here we were, three decades later, still ticking away as a married couple, now with three grown-up boys. Life was comfortable.

But comfortable never seems to last because just as you start to breathe a little easier, life sends you reminders that you should never ever assume things will stay the same. Comfortable was about to blow up in every direction for me.

The "dream job" turned into a living nightmare. It soon became clear I had jumped straight into the middle of a leadership power struggle and with that the most toxic working environment I've ever experienced. The repercussions were big enough to hit the national news! Then, one day, I was called into the office for a meeting with my line manager. I'd had an inkling for quite a while that this day was coming but I'd hoped that, in spite of hating my job, I could hold onto it for the sake of my family.

It wasn't until I was walking to Warren Street station on my way home that it actually hit me: *I'm redundant.* This was about to become the theme that dominated my life over the coming months – *no longer needed or useful.*

As I made my way home on the overcrowded London Underground, I wanted to cry because, with my son's wedding in a couple of months and me being our main household earner, I had no idea how we'd get through. So, I did my usual thing: I went into solution mode and I noticed that I suddenly felt a sense of freedom – something I'd been craving for a long time. 'Be careful what you wish for' springs to mind here.

## Falling apart – the stained glass

It would have been a normal day, except for a family christening. The boys had left earlier to meet their cousins so they could go to the church together. My husband had decided the car needed a wash, so he was out doing that, and I was at home getting ready.

I was in the kitchen, drinking a coffee and taking advantage of this rare quiet time, when my peace was interrupted by the pinging of a text message. As usual, I couldn't find my reading glasses, so I gave up searching and picked up my phone to try to read it, half blind!

*I'm free on Wednesday, all night. What do you think?*

It was from my husband, which didn't make sense. Maybe I needed my glasses after all! After finally finding them, I read it again.

I'd read it right the first time.

It was obviously not meant for me. I was going to be in Manchester on Wednesday for my last business trip, so he knew I wasn't going to be home.

I stood frozen, my mind spinning with all sorts of possible scenarios. Maybe it was meant for his cousin, arranging a men's night out? But deep down I knew what the text meant.

I waited for what seemed forever, just staring at the front door. It used to have a stained-glass window dating back to when the house was built in the 1930s, but the previous owner decided to replace it with plain 1980s crinkled-looking glass. I mean, who would ruin such a work of art? I searched for months for a way to restore it; eventually, my husband found someone who could make something similar, so it was half returned to its former glory. Now that's all I could see, the dark-red stain turning the sunlight into a shade of pink as it passed through the window. I stood waiting for the key to turn, to confront him, and yet there was a sense of calm that even surprised me. It was almost like I'd known this was coming because, over the last year, I'd had this sense something big was about to happen. I'd assumed it was the redundancy but now I knew what it was.

He walked in, dressed in his ill-fitting suit ready for our family day as if nothing was wrong. Then he saw me waiting with the mobile phone in my hand and his smile dropped. It was in that moment that I lost my husband. Standing in front of me was a complete stranger.

When I asked him about the text, he just looked at me with those familiar victim eyes that he could naturally put on whenever he knew he'd done something wrong. And then he said, "I was lonely while you were away working but nothing happened. We were just talking, and I was going to tell her on Wednesday that I'm not interested."

And then he cried, looking to me for comfort, as he always did. I'd become used to this over the years because he was never one to take responsibility and it was always my fault; even his weaknesses were my fault. Needless to say, we didn't go to the christening and it turned out to be a very sad day for our family.

Over the following weeks, he pleaded, cried even, and did all the things a guilty person does. I did what I always did – tried to keep the family together because I knew from experience that divorce can be an ugly thing. My parents' divorce when I was a teenager turned my life upside down and I swore I'd never do that to my own kids. So I was determined to try to work this out and he insisted that "nothing happened!", which I wanted to believe.

Over the following months, I made a conscious effort to remain composed because I was determined not to let the challenges in my life ruin my son's wedding. But it wasn't easy. I'd lost every inch of respect for my husband, and myself.

It wasn't the first time he'd let me down in our marriage, but I thought we'd finally found our groove as a couple. This time, though, things were different. Last time, I had three boys under the age of ten to worry about; now they were grown up, things were different. I was different.

The wedding went well, except for my husband's strange behaviour. He kept getting lost; someone even saw him in the bushes at one point but I just didn't care anymore. When my son's big day was over, and with time to reflect, I found myself thinking about my visit to the doctor a couple of weeks earlier.

It was supposed to be a routine appointment to ask for time off work. The doctor was a young man I hadn't seen before, and he kindly asked me to sit down. When he asked how he could help, I proceeded to tell him about my difficulties at work due to the constant bullying from my boss and the redundancy.

And then, without any warning, tears started streaming down my face.

After a few moments, the doctor leaned in with genuine concern and asked, "Have you had any thoughts of suicide?"

"No, never," I replied, a little confused about his question.

He signed me off and referred me to a counsellor. I left the surgery, relieved that I would never have to return to my workplace again. The door was firmly shut on that drama!

As I drove home, I started mulling over my conversation with the doctor and the shock of being asked if I was suicidal. What really surprised me was that I realised the one person who should have been concerned about me wasn't. Not once since being told about my redundancy had he asked me if I was okay.

Suddenly, those tears returned with a vengeance – so much so I had to pull over to compose myself.

"How could I be married to someone for thirty years and not be able to show him how low I was feeling? And why did I have to pretend I was okay when, actually, I wasn't?" I asked myself.

Then the tears turned into anger. I was furious at how my boss had treated me and felt rage towards my husband. Yet, the most intense feelings were directed inward, towards myself, for allowing these people to treat me as if I was totally dispensable.

In that moment, everything shifted for me. And although I tried to push it aside again for my children, this time it wasn't good enough. The anger I'd felt was becoming harder and harder for me to hide, not least because, since the text message day, my husband hadn't really tried to make amends. It had even got to the point where he felt it appropriate to taunt me with jokes about his indiscretion. He had become like a child who had got away with stealing the last cookie out of the jar! Perhaps years ago, when the kids were little, I would have ignored his ignorance and total disregard for my feelings, but I didn't feel that necessity anymore. So, like a woman on a mission, I resolved to confront him early the next day.

I waited for him to make his coffee and then asked him to sit opposite me in the living room. I was calm, almost emotionless, when I asked, "What's happening here? And I need the truth because I don't want to waste any more of my life."

"I don't know," he replied, with that old, familiar, pitiful look in his eyes.

"You don't know what?" I asked, still showing little emotion.

"I don't know how I feel about you," he elaborated.

And there it was, the answer I needed, the get-out-of-jail-free card. Those few thoughtless words he spoke gave me a sense of clarity I'd not had for a long time. And without a second thought, I replied, "Well, you know what? I know how I feel about you. So, I'd like you to get your stuff and get out of my house." (Actually, I used the F-word but I'll leave that bit out!)

He was clearly shocked. All that arrogance and overconfidence he'd so freely flaunted the past few months seemed to suddenly drain away. Instead of that smug, sly grin, I could see a sense of dread in his eyes. It was the same look I'd seen over the years whenever he had to face any difficulty on his own.

And even though my words were crystal clear, I don't think he quite believed I meant it. He was used to me putting things right, and I guess that's what he was expecting because he stayed frozen in his seat. Sensing his confusion, I spelled it out. "Leave," I said in a controlled voice. And yet, he still looked to me to solve his problem: "But I've got nowhere to go."

"Oh, don't worry," I said. "I'll sort this out for you, just as I have our entire marriage." And with that I went into my office, switched on my laptop and started searching for rooms to let. Within an hour I'd found a room, paid for it and arranged an appointment for him to meet the landlord. I went back downstairs where he was still sitting waiting for me to tell him what to do.

"Okay, I've found you a room, paid for it and the landlord will be there in a minute to let you in."

In the space of a few months, I went from being a woman with a successful career, in a stable marriage with a lovely home to unemployed, single and about to be homeless.

And I was left asking myself, **"How the hell did I get here?"**

## Who am I today?

What struck me the most during this period of my life was how, despite enduring so much loss, I quickly began to feel a profound sense of liberation.

Beneath the grief, loss and betrayal was a sense of space to be myself for the first time in my life. I guess that's what the American Tibetan-Buddhist nun Pema Chödrön meant when she said, "When things fall apart, perhaps they are falling into place."

I may not have planned to end my marriage, sell my home or become jobless, but the universe decided that was what I needed, and it turned out to know what was best for me. Sometimes you get stuck in comfort and refuse to look at your life honestly, so I was lucky to have been startled back to life.

I'm not going to tell you it was easy to put my life back together, because that would be a lie; however, in the process of coming to terms with it all, I created a life that has allowed me to truly embrace who I am and to live on my own terms.

Since my divorce, I've trained to teach mindfulness, I travelled to Nepal to learn about Buddhism, I bought my own home and set up my own business. I've met some incredible people, experienced things I never dreamed possible when I was in my old life and, more importantly, I have an inner sense of peace that is rarely disturbed.

I have built a thriving business working with a diverse range of clients, including those who are facing difficult challenges such as cancer, loss and grief. I also offer a programme called 'The Break-Up' for individuals going through a divorce or separation, whereby I guide my clients towards breaking free from their past patterns and embracing a happier life. Being able to support individuals through their personal challenges is truly an incredible privilege. It not only enriches my own life but also infuses it with profound meaning, which has helped my own healing.

Now, I thought a lot about what to say here because I know you might struggle to find inspiration from what I'm about to share next, but I felt it was important to be honest from the start. In the following pages, I won't be telling you that I met the love of my life and went on to live that happily-ever-after tale.

During my divorce, I started searching for ways to help me deal with my struggles. I read books about moving on from a broken relationship and used the internet to find answers. And what I found was that nearly all the stories I was reading ended with the same "… and then I met a new love and lived happily ever after". I'm not saying there's anything wrong with that but it isn't the only happy ever after and I felt it was time to let people know that happiness doesn't always look like that.

The story I'm about to share is slightly different. It is one of freedom, not the type of freedom so many of us spend our lives striving for – something much more profound. This form of freedom is one whereby I am totally at ease with who I am, and the battle to fit in or to impress others no longer exists. This freedom does not rely on external conditions, because following all the struggles I've had to face, I came to the conclusion that my life was mine to live on my own terms, and that is what I've done.

I want to show you that real happiness doesn't cost anything; nor does it look like what we are told it does. And I want to teach you how to make asking yourself **"What do I want?"** a habit because when you put yourself back into your life, it takes on a whole new meaning.

## Why I wrote this book

I don't know what made you pick up this book, but I'll take a wild guess that it's got something to do with your life not being quite right at the moment. Maybe it's that your relationship is in trouble, or perhaps you are going through a break-up.

It could be that you are feeling a lack of purpose and direction, or maybe there's this nagging feeling that keeps you awake at night but the thought of exploring what's behind it feels too uncomfortable.

Often my clients tell me they aren't creative and don't really have a passion or dream. They might even say, "Anna, you are lucky because you know what you like and want." And this is when we start to look at why they have come to that conclusion, because it is my fundamental belief that we are all born with our unique gifts. It's not that we don't have them; it's that we have forgotten.

When I first started writing this book it was because I wanted an outlet for what was going on in my life at the time and I thought if I shared all my struggles, it would somehow help. So I started writing a memoir, painstakingly going through my life in chronological order.

Then, one day I attended a writing workshop where the presenter talked about something called a 'hybrid' book. If you read self-development books, you'll notice how the writer often weaves in their story with a point they want to make or to give a topic a human context. Well, that, I discovered, is a hybrid book and that is what you'll find in the following pages. A combination of stories from my life and the life of people I've worked with. But because I'm also a realist, I've included some scientific, psychological and philosophical evidence to give the points I raise more substance. However, don't worry – I won't be filling space with academic jargon, because I'd like you to find this book both useful and interesting.

In putting this book together I did a huge amount of research and I asked myself some difficult questions about the things I was discovering. In the end, I reached one overall conclusion: too many of us coast through life, ending up either in situations we don't want to be in or becoming someone we no longer recognise. And what I also discovered is that most of it is not our fault!

This book will explore some important questions about life and human nature that will help you gain a deeper understanding about yourself. It is my hope that by the end you will, at the very least, have gained new insights that will help you decide what you want to do with the rest of your life. And perhaps more importantly, I hope that when you close this book, you will have realised you are holding the key to your freedom – you just forgot where you put it.

However, for us to go forward, we must first go back, and that is where we start – by looking at how you got where you are. And after considering the different aspects that make us who we are, we will explore how to break free from those deeply ingrained beliefs that keep you from being who you really want to be. We live in a society that imposes certain norms and standards, which makes it difficult for us to remain authentic and true to our own identity. Then, one day, we realise we don't even know who we are anymore. And just like I did, you may come to the point of asking yourself: "How did I get here?"

## How to read this book

Before we get started, I'd like to urge you to read the book in order, from front to back, because it is written in a way that will take you through a process of self-inquiry. And as such, one question must be fully explored before moving on to the next. In Part Three, you will find steps you can take to change your life, but for real transformation to happen, you will have to put what is recommended into action.

## Introduction

Oh and I'd recommend you get yourself a notebook so you can complete the exercises and reflections you'll find throughout the book, or you can download the workbook from my website, annazannides.com.

I would also like to suggest that you think of this book as your most trusted friend, by your side, offering you the love and kindness you need to work through your difficulties and come to terms with your life.

So turn off all distractions and find a place where you can be relaxed while you're reading it. Make a commitment to yourself that this won't be a book you just flick through; it will be the stepping stone to your new happier and healthier life.

Before we move on, I'd like to acknowledge that, right now, you might be feeling too sad, angry or confused to see your future in a positive way. However, let me reassure you: if you stick with me, somewhere on the following pages something will jump out at you. It might be a word, a story or a reflection that suddenly resonates with you, and it is there that the shift will start to happen. At the time it might not seem like much, but I can guarantee that once that seed is planted, it will grow.

Just remember, for now, all you need to do is take your time. Let the words sink in, reflect, contemplate and start asking yourself that all-important question: **"What do I want?"**

Are you ready? Yes? Great, let's get started.

## PART ONE

## HOW DID I GET HERE?

As I stepped outside for the first time since the day my marriage ended, I felt the cool breeze of June in London touch my face, and for a moment I forgot the mess that was my life.

I was struggling to do anything normal, like sleeping, getting dressed and holding a conversation that wasn't about my situation. I was living like a zombie, just going through the motions having not quite come to terms with the recent events. It had taken days for me to leave the house. Part of me didn't have the energy and another was too afraid to see people I knew because that would require me to explain what had happened.

But on this day, I quite literally forced myself to step out into the world for the first time since the day I asked my husband to leave.

I got into my car, put the keys into the ignition and reached for a CD, so I could listen to some music as I made my way to the supermarket. Then, as I was about to pull off the drive, I suddenly stopped myself. Yanking the CD out of the player and throwing it to the ground, I shouted, "I don't like this music!"

I instantly reached for a new one, but I still wasn't happy. About twenty minutes later, I found myself sitting in tears looking at the discarded pile of discs on the car floor. Then I cried, "I don't even know what music I like!" And I really didn't.

In her book *Prime Time*, American actor Jane Fonda writes: "In my marriages, I'd lost parts of who I was because I was trying to mould myself into what I thought a man wanted me to be."

In the car that day I realised I had no clue who I was anymore. I'd done exactly what Jane Fonda describes: moulded myself into the wife my husband wanted me to be, the daughter my parents expected me to be and the woman society demanded I should be.

And here I was, a woman in her early fifties, asking myself, **"How did I get here?"**

Now, I am sure that, just like me, you have gone through some unwanted and painful experiences in your life – after all, it's part of the human experience. Sometimes these experiences wake us up to the reality of our lives and although, right now, you might not be able to see it, this thing that's causing you so much trouble at this moment may be the best thing that has ever happened to you. After my life fell apart, I was able to rebuild it with an awareness of the blissful ignorance I had been living in. And while there might not be anything inherently wrong with a little bit of blissful ignorance, unfortunately at some point our denial of the truth will surface somewhere – there is no alternative.

So, whatever has brought you to this point is an opportunity to reset your life. You have been woken from your slumber and however painful that might be right now, you are one of the lucky ones because you have the time to put it right. It's time to stop listening to all those voices that keep telling you who you should be, so you can pay attention to your innermost voice and finally start being who you were always meant to be.

But wait… What if you're not quite sure who that is?

## Who do you want to be?

You may be wondering why I'm asking you who you want to be, rather than what you want to do, so let me clarify. The simple answer is that nothing will change in your life until you allow yourself to be who you truly are, because until then, your internal world will always be in conflict with your external world. And contrary to what society teaches us, a great job, nice house and amazing partner don't guarantee happiness, because as American professor and mindfulness teacher Jon Kabat-Zinn puts it: "Wherever you go, there you are."

However, it is important to remember there was a time when you knew exactly what you wanted and who you were. You only need to watch a child for a day to understand that you were born knowing. But things happened that took your sense of knowing away and somewhere along the line you started being who you were expected to be. As you reflect on your life, it will become apparent that some of the decisions you made were not entirely your own. After all, you had to take into account your parents' expectations, societal norms and a multitude of other influences.

So how much of your life has really been down to what you wanted?

We may think we have free will but that's not completely true because, as you will learn later in this book, we are conditioned away from listening to our inner voice and therefore our decisions or choices are not necessarily our own.

This became very apparent when I found myself single after three decades of marriage. Although things like learning to sleep alone in a double bed again were difficult, nothing could have prepared me for the emotional rollercoaster that lay ahead. To help me manage what I was going through at the time, I started seeing a therapist and it was at one of these sessions that she looked at me and said, "Anna, I've noticed that you have an underlying sadness about you."

That insight unsettled me a bit because up until then I thought I'd done a pretty good job at covering that up. This deep-seated sadness wasn't just because of my divorce or the redundancy or even having to sell my home; it went back much further than that.

I grew up in a family dominated by addiction. My parents' toxic and volatile relationship was fertile ground for breeding insecurity and mistrust. My therapist picked up on my hypervigilance, which she went on to explain was my way of protecting myself – something people do when they grow up in an environment where they don't feel safe. It was a survival instinct that probably served me well as a child. However, it followed me into my adult life, having a detrimental effect on my relationships. This I later understood to be the result of unresolved trauma. That sadness that my therapist noticed was an accumulation of all my experiences. I couldn't trust anyone except myself because I didn't know what that felt like. But over time, I even forgot how to trust myself.

Although therapy offered me an outlet, my discovery of mindfulness and a renewed interest in Buddhism became my anchors.

A few years later, I started teaching mindfulness to people living with cancer. It was through this work that I came to see I wasn't the only one with this underlying sense of sadness. I learned this is a common human experience that is a result of accumulated painful life events, unresolved traumas and disappointments.

For many of the people I worked with, some with incurable cancer, it was the first time they realised how much sadness they were carrying around inside. Often that sadness would turn into anger, especially when people would advise them to "stay positive" – as if being diagnosed with cancer could be turned into something positive!

The point is to realise that this underlying sense of sadness is part of being human. The insistence by some self-improvement gurus that we should always be positive is both toxic and extremely bad for our health.

In 2006, the Dalai Lama gave a talk in which he said, "Buddhism is more than a religion. It is a science of the mind." He went on to say that lasting happiness requires inner peace because happiness without inner peace is "fleeting and superficial". He concluded that to achieve a more stable form of happiness you must train your mind. And contrary to what is commonly thought, true happiness isn't some kind of contrived high; authentic happiness includes our ability to be okay with it all – even, or perhaps especially, the sadness.

This reminds me of an art lesson I once taught. (Don't ask me why a computer science teacher would be teaching art!) Anyway, the topic was 2D and 3D perspective, so to demonstrate I used van Gogh's painting *The Bedroom*. The intention was to show the students how to use angles and shading to create the impression of dimensions. The following picture is an example of perspective drawing, where the lines make us believe that this is not a flat image.

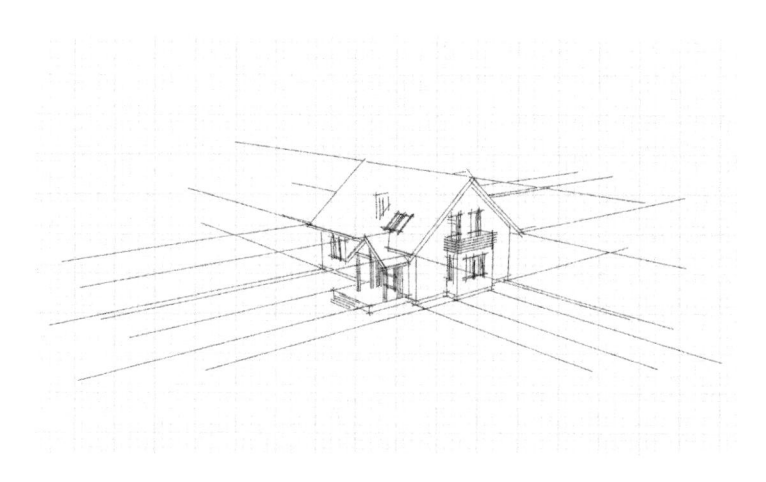

Understanding perspective drawing is useful because it is also how we interpret life. Take this image: if you look at it from above, it will appear differently to, say, looking at it from the side. It might look like a big house, until another bigger house is drawn next to it. And I bet you've formed an opinion – it's in the country perhaps? In fact, it's just lines, isn't it? This is how we live our life, always from a perspective based on where we are standing right now.

Then something traumatic happens to shift or completely dismantle our current view. I had a stark introduction to this the minute I received the text message from my husband. Without any effort, I stopped seeing a trusted partner and in his place was a person I didn't know, and it reopened the lack of trust I already had in others. This is the power of perspective; it's called 'neuroplasticity' in neuroscience and is a fundamental part of Buddhist psychology. We will cover this more later in the book.

For now, if it's not too outrageous, can I ask you to consider the idea that although you may not like or want traumatic and painful experiences, they do serve a purpose. They can be catalysts for better things, if you know how to use them in that way. This is why I focus on helping my clients look at their challenges differently and instead of trying to escape their difficulties, I teach them how to be with them, because real happiness depends on our ability to be okay when things are not okay.

## Real Happiness

When The Dalai Lama was asked what the purpose of life is, he replied, "To be happy."

In early 300 BC, the Greek philosopher Aristotle wrote the *Nicomachean Ethics*, in which he described his view on the purpose of life, concluding that to be an excellent human you must be good at living life. He went on to explain that our highest aim is *eudaimonia* (happiness) and that to achieve *eudaimonia*, you need to have a good character and apply ethics.

So, if happiness is a universal desire, why are so many of us unhappy? And even when we do finally find happiness, it doesn't seem to last for long; it is very fleeting. I'd argue that the reason we struggle with happiness is that we don't know what it is. We certainly know what happiness is as a child, but somewhere along the way it gets lost, and that is down to us being confused about happiness, searching for it somewhere out there, in things and other people.

In one of his talks, Aristotle stated, "The most vulgar would seem to conceive the good and happiness as pleasure, and hence they also like the life of gratification. In this they appear completely slavish, since the life they decide on is a life for grazing animals."

He is talking about how we go about our lives addicted to temporary pleasures in the hope they will make us happy, and yet that doesn't seem to work.

Even though those words were written long before modern technology and mass production, human behaviour doesn't seem to have changed much. To make matters worse, today, pleasure and instant gratification are only one click away. And despite all our progress as a human race, it seems we are less happy than our ancestors. In 2020, Samaritans reported that 4,912 people had died by suicide that year in England alone. That's an annual suicide rate of ten people per 100,000. And, what's more alarming, for men between the age of 45 and 49, the rate goes up to 23.8 per 100,000. If we take into account these increasingly bleak statistics around poor mental health, we might begin to see the way we are living our lives isn't good for us.

Aristotle taught that to achieve true happiness we must be serious about living well. He went on to say that happiness is a type of work, something we must take seriously. He believed true happiness cannot be found only by seeking pleasure. Aristotle explained that the function of humans is to engage in activities that are guided or necessitated by reason, which are ultimately expressions of the soul.

What we can learn from Aristotle is that to be happy, we must consciously work towards creating a life where we can be happy; it doesn't just happen. We can choose to follow a life chasing pleasure, or we can commit to creating a life based on living well with high moral standards.

However, while Aristotle makes some good points, the Buddha's view differs. The Buddha taught that to be happy, we must focus on developing a stable mind and to live what is often called 'the middle way'. This means that to be happy is to learn to be content and less reliant on temporary pleasures. We are encouraged to be happy with and without the objects of our desires. This way, our happiness is not dependent on our circumstances. I understand that this may sound unattainable, but please bear with me for a moment because, as I delve further, it will become clearer and feel more achievable.

The Dalai Lama explains it this way: "We can never obtain peace in the outer world until we make peace with ourselves."

Here, the Dalai Lama makes the point that real happiness is not something we can buy, nor is it something we can get from things and other people. This doesn't mean that we must live a life of poverty or never experience pleasure. However, it is the degree by which our happiness depends on these pleasures that causes so much difficulty in our life. Addiction is defined as an insatiable hunger, and while we may not see pleasure seeking as an addiction, if we look closely at how our life is dictated by our constant chasing after pleasure, we may see how it causes us to be unhappy – quite the opposite of what we want.

I grew up believing that as long as I had certain conditions in my life, I'd be happy. I also thought that to be a good parent, you had to give your children everything and to make their lives perfect.

At the height of my career, I got so swept up in it that, one time, when I was feeling rich, I bought a house and a car on the same day. You might think there's nothing wrong with that – after all, I was working hard, so why not treat myself? But none of that was really mine. To buy the house, I needed a bigger mortgage, and I had to take out a loan for the car, but I thought I could afford them. What I didn't realise was that the more I bought, the more trapped I was becoming, because the more money I spent, the harder I had to work. And this is how we get stuck in the cycle of work–buy–work more–buy more. For some, that might be perfectly fine, but for many of us this becomes the very thing we are desperate to escape from.

In 1943, Abraham Maslow published his paper 'A Theory of Human Motivation'. Maslow is mostly known for what is widely called the 'hierarchy of needs', which has become a popular framework in sociology research, management training and education. It is commonly represented as a pyramid.

Let's briefly look at Maslow's theory:

## Maslow's Hierarchy of Needs

**Self-Actualisation**
Fulfillment, Living to One's Full Potential

**Esteem**
Respect, Self-Esteem, Status, Recognition, Strength, Freedom

**Love and Belonging**
Friendship, Intimacy, Family, Sense of Connection

**Safety Needs**
Security of Body, Employment, Resources, Health, Property

**Physiological Needs**
Air, Food, Water, Shelter, Sleep, Clothing, Sex (Reproduction)

*PSYCHOLOGICAL/SPIRITUAL* — *MATERIAL*

The first level of Maslow's hierarchy focuses on our **Physiological** needs. It's a given that we all need to breathe, eat, drink and sleep. However, interestingly, Maslow is said to have included sex at the primal level of our basic needs. But as we will discuss later in the book, this isn't necessarily essential for our survival, except as a need for breeding.

In addition, his theory is used to explain human motivation – for example, when we don't have food, we will be more motivated to do whatever we can to satisfy our hunger. At the **Safety** level, we are motivated by our need to feel safe, and this requires us to live in a secure environment where we do not feel constantly threatened. This also includes a certain level of security around our source of income so we can create a safe environment for ourselves and our family. Once we have our basic survival needs met and we feel safe, Maslow argued that to improve our sense of happiness, we want to feel we belong and that we are loved. Hence, he added a level he called **Love and Belonging**.

The top two levels, **Esteem** and **Self-Actualisation**, go beyond our instinctive survival needs and because of that they are more complex.

However, science isn't foolproof and often needs to be taken in the context of how the evidence was collected. In Maslow's case, it must be noted that his sample was made up of what he called 'the master race', which included people like Albert Einstein and Eleanor Roosevelt. He is even quoted as saying, "The study of crippled, stunted, immature and unhealthy specimens can yield only a cripple psychology and a cripple philosophy." His research was focused on studying only 1% of the healthiest college student population. If we put this into context, we can see the huge limitations of his findings and the extreme bias.

Further, there is no real evidence that Maslow intended his research to be interpreted as a pyramid or that he was implying that we must achieve one layer before we can successfully move on to the next. In fact, if that was the case, rich people would be happy all the time and the poor would never experience happiness.

While establishing a definitive correlation between wealth and happiness proves challenging, several studies highlight an intriguing trend. In economically disadvantaged countries, individuals frequently find greater happiness when their basic needs are fulfilled. In contrast, in wealthier nations, where fundamental necessities are easily accessible, people tend to prioritise more meaningful pursuits in their search for happiness. This observation aligns with Maslow's theory, which suggests that once our basic needs are satisfied, we naturally gravitate towards activities that fill our lives with a sense of purpose.

To put this into context, I'd like to share the following story from when I visited Nepal, which happens to be one of the poorest countries in the world.

## Happiness is relative

Perhaps one of the biggest impacts my divorce had was on the family structure. We went from one neat unit to pieces here and there. And although my marriage might not have been ideal, my family was my foundation. My home was where I knew I'd find my children at the end of a hard day. So when that was suddenly gone, I was forced to face an empty nest without any prior preparation.

Not knowing what I wanted or who I was anymore, I decided to book myself a flight to Nepal to attend a Buddhist retreat. Up to this point my interest in

Buddhism was something I'd kept to myself because it just wasn't the thing to do as a good Greek girl. But I knew it was time for me to do what I wanted, to listen to the voice I had ignored for most of my life. So I left my "normal" suburban London life to travel alone to the other side of the world with no idea of what I'd find there. I thought I should climatise before checking into the monastery, so I started my trip with a few days in a beautiful guest house located just outside Kathmandu. Bouddha is a busy place of pilgrimage for Tibetans, with a huge Buddhist stupa at the centre of the lively town.

And it was there that a young man gave me a different perspective on happiness.

One morning as I sat on the lawn drinking my freshly brewed coffee, feeling anxious as I watched the monkeys running on the rooftop of the small dining room, silently hoping they wouldn't pounce on me, I noticed a young man sprawled on the floor, fixing the doorway of the kitchen. I couldn't be precise about his age because the harshness of that way of life can make people look older than their years. He was a small, fragile-looking man whose disability meant he had little use of his lower body. I was intrigued at how, despite his obvious physical challenges, he was still able to move so easily.

When he'd finished his work, he came and sat next to me and then, with a smile, he said hello. I was taken aback by the fluency of his English, apparent self-confidence and eloquence. I was also surprised to see a sparkle in his eyes rather than the dullness I expected from someone who must have endured such hardship in his life.

I asked him how he was, and we started to chat. He went on to tell me he had been born with muscular dystrophy and could only walk with the aid of sticks. He was grateful for the work the locals gave him. I wanted to know more about this remarkable man, so I asked him if he would tell me a little bit about himself, which he was more than happy to do. I guess it's not often someone shows such an interest in him.

"I was born in India and my family are poor. I'm married with a young daughter," he explained.

"Why did you come to Nepal?" I asked.

"Well, my wife is blind, and I wanted to give my daughter the chance to go to school."

"And Nepal gives you this opportunity?" I asked.

"Yes, it's better here. At least here we have a tent to live in on a compound and I can work to feed my family."

There was no anger in his tone, nor resentment, and I wondered how anyone could maintain this level of contentment with so little to be thankful for.

"But I am happy," he said as if reading my mind.

He was happy? I wasn't sure I could believe that. What did he have to be happy about?

The next day, as I was walking back to the guest house after my morning walk around the stupa, I noticed the young man sitting on the step of a shop in conversation with someone who looked like a Westerner, most likely a traveller. This time he was fixing shoes. *Obviously a very resourceful person*, I thought. They were laughing and carrying on with life as if they had no cares in the world, oblivious to the poverty around them.

A few days later, I met a young lady who was running a small, very basic coffee shop outside the monastery I had moved to. At night she would take out a mattress and sleep on the shop floor so she could catch the early morning trade. About three days into my retreat, when I'd gone out for a coffee, she looked at me and said, "I don't understand you Westerners. What do you come here for?"

She thought we were crazy leaving our comforts to travel to a poverty-stricken country in search of answers, in the hope we could finally be happy, when people like her would swap lives with us in an instant. Here she was, living the most basic of basic lives, sleeping in the doorway, on a concrete floor, so she could sell a few coffees to the lost souls who didn't know just how lucky they were. *What irony*, I thought, *she thinks we have the answers to happiness, and we spent thousands to find it on her doorstep.*

This is when I realised that happiness is relative – not dependent on what we have, not necessarily even our living conditions, but very dependent on our attitude. Viktor Frankl, a renowned professor of psychiatry and a survivor of Auschwitz concentration camp, wrote in his book *Man's Search For Meaning*: "When we are no longer able to change a situation, we are challenged to change ourselves."

That young man in Nepal taught me the importance of acceptance and gratitude. Even though he had no material wealth and was born with a crippling disability, he had a strength I'd rarely seen before.

And that young lady in the coffee shop made me realise that despite all the resources I had, I would not let myself be happy. Somewhere on this journey of life I had pushed myself to the side so I could assume the roles that had been designed for me. And I took these roles on with such conviction that eventually I had no idea who I was. This is what we call 'conditioning' or 'unconscious living'.

## Losing ourselves in unconscious living

There are two schools of thought that I'd like you to think about for a moment. The first is the idea that we are what we inherit – in other words, our biology. Its main premise is that we come with a set of genes that determine our characteristics and behaviour and, as such, we are predetermined. This approach has its roots in biological science, which was mostly theoretical up to the late 1800s. In 1865, Gregory Mendel, known as the father of genetics, introduced the fundamental laws of inheritance. Later, scientists went on to research

DNA, and today it's pretty much accepted that we are the result of specific genes that come together, inherited from our ancestors. These genes literally make us; they determine the colour of our skin, eyes, height and so on. Of course, I am not going to attempt to go into any kind of detail here. I just want you to start thinking about how some things are just out of your control.

The science of human behaviour is another ideology that focuses on our biological makeup. However, its main argument is that our character traits and behaviour are also inherited. Now this is where it gets interesting but rather disturbing. The relationship between behaviour and genetics was first talked about in the late 1800s by English scientist Sir Francis Galton, who happened to be a cousin of Charles Darwin. Both scientists concluded that mental powers run in the family. In fact, the term 'nature and nurture' was first coined by Galton.

Scientists then went on to conduct experiments on twins to come up with an almost universal view that intelligence is inherited, and that some people are predisposed to becoming successful or criminal. As recently as 1969, scientists such as Arthur Jenson were adamant that the average IQ of Black Americans was significantly lower than White Americans. He even went as far as saying that 80% of intelligence is inherited. Let's think about the implications of this sort of science on the psyche of Black people and on the Whites who grew up thinking they were superior. Science has a lot to answer for!

On the other hand, scientists such as Freud argued that we are products of our environment, and that this determines how well we perform in school and in our social life. Maslow's theory is an example of this nurture-based psychology.

In Freud's theory of psychosexual stages of development he describes a child's feelings of desire for his or her opposite-sex parent and jealousy and anger towards his or her same-sex parent. This theory asserts that a boy feels he is competing with his father for the possession of his mother, while a girl feels she is competing with her mother for her father's affections. This is called the 'Oedipus complex'. The term 'Electra complex' was introduced by Carl Jung to describe how this manifests in girls. Freud proposed the concept that females suffer from penis envy. However, in 1926, feminist psychoanalyst Karen Horney disputed Freud's claims, adding that men had womb envy.

This is just a little reminder that neither science nor psychology are ever unbiased; in fact, they are usually driven by political or business agendas. It is therefore important that when we use certain theories, we remember they are not fact. Generally, the nurture argument tends to incline towards the left of the political spectrum, while the nature scenario is more right-leaning. Historically, both science and psychology have been dominated by White males, who went about to prove or disprove hypotheses they believed to be right or wrong, making their findings extremely subjective.

Why is this relevant, and why am I sharing this with you here? Well, the problem is that these arguments and theories have influenced how we are raised, the roles we play in society and what we believe about ourselves. We have been conditioned based on the words of a few privileged White men, and unfortunately this continues today.

The point I want to leave you with here is that for real change to happen, you need to become aware of the role conditioning plays in your life. Society is modelled around popular scientific and psychological theories that shape our institutions and how we educate and parent our children. It dictates the roles that women and men play and writes the social narrative we base our views on. Over time, all these stories set out what is acceptable, expected and "normal" until we forget who we are so we can fit into those social norms.

And yet, despite all that conditioning, there is a part of you that lies waiting to be expressed and acknowledged because it cannot be erased, only obscured from view. This unexpressed part of you is what we call the 'authentic self' and because it is trapped inside, it can surface as sadness, anger, depression, emptiness and dissatisfaction.

In his book *Rebel Buddha: A Guide to a Revolution of Mind*, Dzongchen Ponlop Rinpoche, a highly respected Buddhist teacher, writes: "Our lifestyle is our expression of who we are, determined by our psychologies and past histories. You need to know who you are so you can create a life you fit in."

And in her book *The Art of Memoir*, Mary Karr writes that if we do not confront our past, it will continue to tug at us without us being aware of it happening. She adds: "Nobody can be autonomous in making choices today unless she grasps how she's being internally yanked around by stuff that came before."

## Section summary

### Key points:

- It is part of the human condition to experience an underlying sadness.
- We experience life from the perspective of where we are at any given moment.
- Happiness is relative, dependent on our views and perspective.
- Happiness is less reliant on external conditions and much more to do with attitude.
- Happiness is not the same as pleasure, which is fleeting.
- Although scientists and psychologists have given us useful interpretations, we must remember that they are often subjective and changeable views.
- Our past plays a part in our present, especially if we do not face it.

It's important we start recognising how our past is still very much right here in our present, controlling how we live our lives, who we think we are and affecting the quality of our lives. If you are lucky enough to have grown up relatively unscathed by the adults in your life, then your past will hopefully be a positive influence, but I have a funny feeling that you are not one of those lucky ones. Or perhaps nobody can be completely free from a past that has dented their self-image.

### Reflection on past conditioning

It's time to grab yourself a warm drink and find your notepad or the downloadable workbook. Now, spend a bit of time writing down whatever has stuck out for you so far. Find a comfortable, quiet place and just write or draw anything you feel needs to be expressed right now. Don't judge or edit – it is for your eyes only.

When you are finished writing or drawing, I want you to reflect on this question:

**Who do I want to be?**

A useful way to do this type of reflection is through a contemplative meditation. This can be done by sitting, lying down or walking mindfully and allowing the question "Who do I want to be?" to flow. The trick is not to begin searching for an answer, because that will shut down possibilities.

> It is better to be curious but not fixed in your view. Give yourself a time limit – ten or twenty minutes, or longer if you are a seasoned meditator.
>
> Make sure you have your notepad next to you so you can jot down anything that jumps out at you.
>
> If you find this difficult or want help to work through the reflections in this book, you can find additional resources on my website, annazannides.com.

Okay, are you ready to continue? Great, let's do this.

## Forgetting Who You Are

Did you know we spend approximately 30% of our life sleeping and 47% of our waking time not paying attention?

This means we are only present for 23% of our life, and therefore we make many decisions while we are distracted. We then wonder why we take wrong paths or end up with people who aren't good for us. To begin to make more conscious choices about your life, you must develop the capacity to notice what you are doing, when you are doing it.

This tendency to be distracted explains why when something traumatic happens to us it can also lead to sudden clarity. Humans are built to react quickly when in danger, and trauma sends a distress signal to our brain in the same way as being in danger. If you are going through difficulty, such as an illness, redundancy or a relationship ending, you might even feel a sense of awareness you didn't have before. This is because you are experiencing something new and, therefore, you can't just be on autopilot; you need to use a new neurological pathway. For example, have you ever noticed that when you are driving somewhere you go to often, sometimes you get to your destination without remembering how, but when you are driving somewhere you've never been before, you are completely focused? This is because your brain can't draw on stored information – it's not in your memory yet.

The more we do something, the more able we are to do it without thinking. We build a reserve of automated actions – commonly referred to as habits. This explains why we spend so much of our time not being present – because we don't have to pay attention. Of course, there's a purpose for this: we must learn to do certain things automatically, like how to brush our teeth and make a coffee, otherwise life would be unmanageable. What we are not supposed to do is live most of our days in this state of distraction and autopilot, because the danger is that one day we may look back on our life and wonder where it went.

And this is why mindfulness is so important. We need to raise our level of self-awareness so we can be fully engaged in our lives.

## The role of mindfulness

I trained to teach mindfulness shortly after my divorce. In the beginning I worked primarily with people living with cancer, bereavement and loss. Nowadays I work more broadly, which includes working with schools, workplaces and individuals, all looking to improve their well-being.

When Jon Kabat-Zin started to explore the idea of using mindfulness meditation with his patients to help them cope with stress, pain and illness, he wanted to reduce the high rate of reoccurrence. Kabat-Zin was a student of renowned mindfulness teacher Thich Nhat Hanh and he wanted to use what he had learned to see if it would help people living with stress and other mental health issues, because he was troubled by the high rate of relapse in those that completed therapy.

Today, mindfulness has become a popular alternative or complementary method used to help people from all walks of life, suffering with a variety of challenges. And there is increasing evidence showing its benefits. However, as it is currently an unregulated industry, it isn't always taught correctly and as such can get bad press. Thankfully there is now a mindfulness teachers register and agreed standards for those who meet the criteria, so it's likely that, at some point, mindfulness will become a little more regulated – well, that's my hope.

## So what is mindfulness, and why is it relevant to us here?

To answer the question "How did I get here?" and, perhaps more importantly, to be able to answer the question "Who am I, really?" you will need to get to know your own mind. And that can only happen when you learn to pay attention. It is through introspection that you begin to recognise how your past is playing out in your present and therefore determining your future. You cannot break free if you do not know what is keeping you stuck in the past or repeating patterns that are not good for you.

When you think about mindfulness, what comes to mind? Is it that it helps to make you calmer? To an extent, that might be true in the short term. However, what you will notice if you practise for a while is that you begin to become familiar with your thought habits. You might also notice how self-critical you are or pessimistic or even always optimistic.

Why is that important? Because when you get to know how your mind works, you will have a much better understanding of what drives you to be who you think you are. And you might be surprised at what you discover.

But what is this thing we call 'the mind'?

## Defining the mind

Aristotle thought the brain was merely a radiator that kept the all-important heart from overheating. In fact, Aristotle believed that our consciousness, imagination and memory were rooted in the human heart. Then, in approximately 170 BC, Roman physician Galen suggested the brain was more complex, and it was where thought, personality and bodily functions were stored.

Later, in 16th-century Belgium, anatomist Andreas Vesalius created a highly detailed map of the nervous system. In 1791, Luigi Galvani showed that the nervous system was controlled by electric pulses. Then in 1932, Sir Charles Sherrington and Edgar Adrian advanced our understanding of the central nervous system. And in 1963, Sir John Eccles showed how neurons communicate through electrical and chemical signalling.

Despite the progress made in neuroscience to understand the brain, there was still the question of what activates the electrons. In spiritual traditions, this question is answered by the idea of a 'consciousness'. But science has struggled to prove its existence, and while we may understand the workings of the brain better, we have yet to locate consciousness.

In 1649, the French philosopher René Descartes came up with the influential idea that while the brain may control the body, the mind is something intangible – distinct from the brain – where the soul and thoughts reside.

Until recently, science considered the brain and mind to be one of the same, which is something that Buddhism has always refuted. Neuroscientist Rick Hanson defines the mind as the information within the brain. He explains that just as the heart's main function is to move blood around our body, the brain's main function is to move information around. Hanson asserts that when your brain changes, your mind changes and you can do this deliberately through applied mindfulness and meditation. This rewiring of the brain is called neuroplasticity.

So is it possible that the mind and the brain are not the same? While researching for this book, I became intrigued by the work of quantum physicist David Bohm. I will not attempt to explain such a complex theory as quantum physics here, but I think it is useful for you to have a basic idea of what it is. Simply put, quantum physics tries to explain how everything works; it focuses on atoms, matter, particles and energy. David Bohm studied various aspects of quantum physics, concluding that science can never fully explain the world.

Motivated by this, he embarked on an exploration of the spiritual realm, engaging in profound discussions with the renowned philosophical teacher Jiddu Krishnamurti. Through extensively documented debates, it became increasingly evident that Bohm had come to accept the likelihood of the existence of consciousness, even though science could not yet provide definitive verification.

Although Einstein didn't study consciousness, he did express some thoughts on the matter in his personal writings and conversations with colleagues. One notable quote attributed to Einstein is "Consciousness is a fundamental reality, just like space and time. But we are still very far from a comprehensive understanding of it."

This statement suggests Einstein believed consciousness to be a fundamental aspect of reality. However, he also acknowledged that our understanding of consciousness is limited and there is much more to learn about this complex and mysterious phenomenon.

We can summarise that there are three elements to contemplate when attempting to define the mind. Firstly, the brain is a tangible organ that manages our physical body. Secondly, Rick Hanson suggests that the mind controls the brain. Lastly, if the mind isn't a physical organ, it may be equivalent to what we frequently refer to as consciousness. This definition aligns with Buddhist teachings.

It's important to talk about the difference between the mind and brain so you can see how powerful your thoughts are. If science and Buddhism are right, then it's crucial that we learn how to take some control over our thoughts and mind.

## Section summary

### Key points:

- The mind and the brain are not the same.
- The mind plays a prominent role in how we interpret the world around us; it drives our decisions and choices.
- To change our external world, we must start by changing our internal world.

So if our thoughts are the source of everything, then the answer to our problems lies in altering our thoughts. The following diagram is a simple illustration of how it all works.

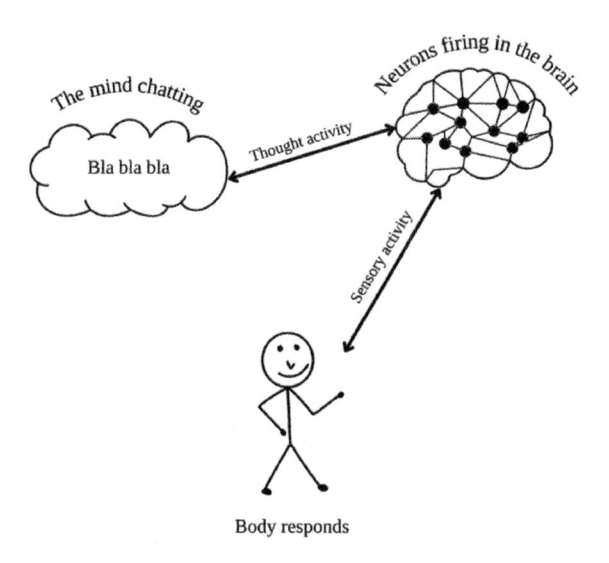

*The mind chatting* — Bla bla bla ← Thought activity — Neurons firing in the brain ← Sensory activity — Body responds

The important point to take from what we've covered in the previous pages is that there is more to life than we humans can prove – even some of the most renowned scientists reached that conclusion. And if that is the case, then perhaps we can also accept that there is more to being human than we can really imagine. You may not realise it yet, but you do not have to be the victim of your past or your external conditions, because you are the creator of your life. And I'm not talking in a New Age, spiritual way – it's science!

But if we are the ones creating our lives, why aren't we all living amazing lives? And why are so many of us unhappy or lost?

Let's see if we can answer these questions.

## How we become who we are

In her book *The Top Five Regrets of The Dying*, Bronnie Ware found the number one regret of the dying was that they wished they "had the courage to live a life true to myself, not the life others expected of me".

She goes on to explain that when people look back at their lives, they often mourn the fact they will die without fully realising their dreams and that this is because of the choices they made along the way. And it's only when their health begins to decline that they truly comprehend the significance of good health.

So, what makes us give up on ourselves?

As the French philosopher Jean-Paul Sartre said: "We only become what we are by the radical and deep-seated refusal of that which others have made of us."

According to Aristotle, by the age of seven we have firmly become who we will be. He is famously known for saying "Give me a child until he is seven and I will show you the man."

What did he mean by this?

In those first few years, we form a belief of who we are based on both nature and nurture. Theories such as those of the pioneering developmental psychologist and psychiatrist John Bowlby suggest that our future is determined by our early relationship with our mother. If we did not form a strong attachment, or if our mother was somehow absent, we are more likely to develop insecurities as adults. Bowlby's attachment theory can be summarised as follows:

- We are born with an innate need to form a strong bond with one main attachment figure; this is called 'monotropy'. Bowlby suggested this one relationship was more important than any other.
- We are biologically pre-programmed to form attachments with others as a survival instinct.
- A child's attachment should be formed by the age of two and a half or, at the latest, by the age of five for them to grow up emotionally healthy.
- Bowlby's maternal deprivation hypothesis states that continual disruption of attachment between the infant and primary caregiver could lead to long-term cognitive, social and emotional difficulties in adulthood.
- He then suggests that those early years become the prototype for all future social relationships.

Based on the views of both Bowlby and Aristotle, we might conclude that we are victims of our childhood. However, humans have an innate ability to adapt and evolve. This is how we survive in a world that is constantly changing. In addition, research that began in the 1950s shows us that the human body is largely replaced by new cells at least every decade. We only need to look in the mirror to see that we are not the same person we were a decade ago, maybe a year ago or possibly even last week!

So are we really victims of our past, or do we just think we are?

## How our self-belief is formed

Historically, most mental health problems were attributed to God as an act of punishment for the person's sins. Equally, someone who displayed mental health issues was seen as under the influence of magic, witchcraft or evil spirits. And the treatment of people who were living with any form of mental health problem was often harsh and inhumane. Fortunately, things have changed. We now have a better understanding of what causes poor mental health. And it is almost always the outcome of some sort of trauma. Put simply, our mental well-being is directly affected by our suffering. When it is severe or prolonged, the damage can have a devastating impact on our mental and social wellness.

In 1895, Sigmund Freud said, "I think this man is suffering from memories," acknowledging the idea that trauma is caused by an event in our life and held in our body, creating memories.

Bessel van der Kolk wrote a comprehensive account of his experience working with people affected by traumatic stress, also known as post-traumatic stress disorder (PTSD); in his book *The Body Keeps the Score: Brain, Mind, and Body in the Healing of Trauma* he writes: "We have learned that trauma is not just an event that took place sometime in the past; it is also the imprint left by that experience on the mind, brain and body. This imprint is ongoing."

He goes on to confirm his view that "trauma isn't all in one's head".

Kolk sparked some controversy when he questioned the effectiveness of talking therapy. Although he acknowledges that it provides trauma victims with a platform to voice their experiences, he notes that it doesn't necessarily alter the body's responses. In his view, talking therapy doesn't convince the body that it's no longer in harm's way, which is the case with unaddressed trauma.

Kolk states that for real change to happen, the body needs to learn that the danger has passed, and he suggests the way to do that is to learn to live in the reality of the present.

His research has given us a better understanding of trauma and the process of healing.

Today we know that many mental health disorders are associated with a chemical imbalance, caused by stress hormones. Common treatments now include one or a combination of medication, therapy and alternative approaches such as mindfulness.

It's crucial to have some awareness of trauma since it's probable you've encountered it in some form. The most prevalent type of trauma often involves some sort of loss, which we'll delve into more later. It's important to recognise that trauma can take various forms and can have diverse impacts on your life.

Kolk emphasises that our bodies retain trauma, and failing to address it may result in mental health problems and physical illnesses.

To expand on what we've discussed so far, let's look at something called 'epigenetics' by answering these questions:

Do we inherit trauma, and is it in our genes?

In 2005, Bruce Lipton published *The Biology of Belief: Unleashing the Power of Consciousness, Matter & Miracles*, which is the result of years of research on the nature of life, in particular our genes and cells. He starts his book by asking: "If you could be anybody, who would you be?" He then goes on to say that he spent an obsessive amount of time thinking about this question because he really didn't like who he was and he wanted to change his identity.

Even though Lipton had a good career as a cell biologist and was a medical school professor at the time, his personal life was, as he describes, "a shambles" and the more he tried to find happiness, the more unhappy he became. When he was offered the opportunity to leave mainstream academia to begin working for an independent medical college, he gained the freedom to explore his own beliefs about the nature of life.

It was there he noticed something that would change his life. While he was reviewing his research, he suddenly realised "that a cell's life is controlled by the physical and energetic environment and not by its genes". Lipton ultimately concluded that the mechanisms of life are initiated not by genes, but by a single cell's consciousness of its surroundings.

Why are Lipton's findings important? Well, for one, they tell us our lives are not determined by our genes but by our responses to the environment we live in and this contradicts the idea that we are destined to live by the genes we inherit.

Lipton declares, "I realised that there was a science-based path that would take me from my job as a perennial victim to my new position as co-creator of my destiny."

Epigenetics goes even further: it also deduces that the character of our life is based on how we perceive it. This is called 'signal transduction' and argues that we have the capability to shape our biology through our perceptions.

What the likes of Lipton are proving is that we are more a product of our environment than of our genes, supporting nurture over nature. Even Darwin, the father of evolution, conceded in his later life that he had not given enough credit to the role of nurture in his findings.

## How we are conditioned

There is a common narrative that you have probably been taught from the time you were born. It may vary depending on where you grew up and even your cultural background but generally in the so-called developed countries, it is similar.

In your community, you likely heard the same storyline from the adults who cared for you, the TV programmes you watched, the conversations you were exposed to and the songs you listened to. This lifetime narrative became your blueprint without you even noticing. The storyline most people grow up believing looks something like this:

**Linear Life**

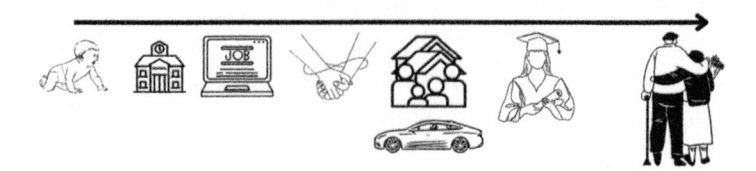

1. Get a good education so you can get a secure job.
2. A secure job leads to stability and happiness.
3. Meet a compatible significant other, fall in love and commit to a lifelong relationship.
4. Set up home, get a car, have children, go on holidays and experience eternal happiness.
5. Work hard so you can retire and enjoy life, if you make it that far!

One way or another, this story has been our collective narrative for centuries, and to a certain degree it makes perfect sense, especially when we remember Maslow's hierarchy of needs. However, as we often learn as we grow older, life is not linear, nor does it always go to plan. Life is unpredictable, unreliable and mostly out of our control.

Doesn't life look more like this?

## Real Life

I would argue that investing so much of our life trying to create this ideal is what causes so much dissatisfaction.

The fact that we are constantly chasing after things and people in the hope they will make us happy is the very reason we are unable to be truly happy. And isn't that a risky way to live, considering all the things we rest our worth and happiness on can be lost in an instant?

In her book *Welcoming the Unwelcome: Wholehearted Living in a Brokenhearted World*, Pema Chödrön writes, "Never underestimate the power of the mind. How you work with things really can transform what seems to be. Working with the inner can transform the outer – though not in any linear way that you can put your finger on."

## Section summary

### Key points:

- Epigenetics shows us that genes are changed by the environment.
- We are not victims of our genes.
- We have the capability to recreate ourselves and therefore our life.

Both epigenetics and neuroscience show us that we can reprogramme our neuropathways to break free from our old habits. This isn't new – the Buddha taught that our thoughts become our reality; in other words, we create what we experience.

So, if we are such powerful beings, with the capacity to create wonderful, meaningful lives, why is it that so many of us live mundane, often unfulfilling lives? Well, I'd argue it's because we are conditioned to forget just how powerful we really are. This is something we explore throughout this book because if you can learn something, you can also unlearn it, and there begins the transformation.

As we have already discussed, it's possible that we have been approaching things the wrong way. So instead of depending on the external world, perhaps we should concentrate on getting our internal world in order. That's why in the next section I'd like to introduce the concept of authenticity.

## Authenticity

Before I became aware of the importance of authenticity, I believed that to be happy I had to live my life according to the fairy tales I was taught as a child. And although I finished school with no qualifications and then went on to college for another three years to finally end my education with very little to show for it, I continued to try to fit into those social norms.

I was always looking for the next career break and then once I got it, I'd get bored and would leave. I tried hard to fit in and do the "right" thing, but it never felt right for me. My internal world was always in conflict with the reality I was living in, and I was never sure if I was doing what I wanted to do or what was expected of me, because it was all so confusing.

Despite knowing that all I wanted was freedom, I still ended up getting married. I never felt that staying single and pursuing a different life was a real option. So I gave up my true passions to settle down, as this was how I was brought up – to believe this was the best thing for me. Now I'm not saying I shouldn't have got married, and I certainly don't regret having children; however, I do wonder whether my decisions were ever conscious choices or pre-programmed reactions.

After all, how does a naturally free-spirited, slightly rebellious, strong-minded young woman still slip into the trap of following this linear ideal of life? How did she fall for this happily-ever-after story? Well maybe it's because everything, from the time we are born, pushes us in that direction. And because we have this innate need to fit in and be part of the clan, it makes sense to do what most other people do.

But the sad truth is that when we follow a path that is set out for us, rather than the path that calls to us from our innermost depth, we cause a huge conflict. And over time, not only do we let go of our dreams, we also forget who we are at our core and perhaps never really get to know our true purpose.

Mind you, this doesn't happen without a fight; that's what the teenage years are all about – our last cry for the freedom to be ourselves. My last freedom cry happened a little earlier. It was at the young age of nine and it came to me in an unexpected way.

## The promise

It was just an ordinary school day and I was sat at my desk. I was supposed to be listening to my teacher but, as usual, I was lost in a daydream, staring out the window, wishing I could be outside playing rather than stuck in a classroom forced to listen to words that I had no interest in.

And then, without any warning, my daydream was interrupted.

"Promise you'll never forget."

Although the voice was familiar, it still startled me. I looked around to see where the voice had come from. It didn't seem to have come from anywhere and nobody else seemed to have noticed.

Then I heard it again.

"Promise you'll never forget," it repeated, this time with more intensity.

Too young to really understand what was going on, I sat still, trying to work it out until eventually I realised that to make the voice go away, I had to respond.

"I promise I won't forget," I whispered, hoping my classmates wouldn't hear and make fun of me.

Then, just as quickly as the voice came, it left.

Over the years, I've tried to work out what I was supposed to remember but it wasn't until that incident in the car just after my divorce that it made sense. In her book *The Truth Will Set You Free, But First It Will Piss You Off!: Thoughts on Life, Love and Rebellion*, Gloria Steinem writes: "Female humans may be more ourselves before we are ten or so, before gender expectations kick in, and perhaps again after we have passed the age of having and raising children."

It was evident that I was too outspoken and not feminine enough, and because of that I was often called a tomboy. I was too ambitious and driven to fit in, so somewhere along the line I realised I'd have to pretend to be just like all the other good girls. That voice was supposed to serve as my reminder that I should always remember who I am at my core, and yet even with that early awareness of what was going on, I still got lost.

Research conducted by psychologists Piaget, Kohlberg and Erikson found that between the ages of five and twelve, when our circle of influence expands, and we are fully immersed in the education system, we start to compare ourselves to our peers. This is when we start to worry about what others think of us and develop an intrinsic need to be liked.

They found that by the age of five, we start to ask ourselves: "Who do others want me to be?", whereas when we are younger, we quite frankly don't care. It is at this age that we turn to the adults in our life for confirmation that we are doing the right thing and we look towards our peers for acceptance, slowly becoming the person others expect us to be. Except of course during our teenage years, which is our last attempt at salvaging that authentic part of ourselves.

The question then becomes, how do we stay true to ourselves in a world that is hell bent on making us all fit into the same box and where being different is shunned rather than appreciated?

Carl Jung argued that each of us has an innate individuality and that we come into this world with a specific character. He went on to say that our goal in life is to become ourselves, to realise our authentic self and to do that we must express our inner world. The extent to which we can align our outer world with our inner world determines the quality of our life. In short, what Jung taught us is that when we are unable to express our uniqueness, we create a constant battle with our external world. Authenticity helps us live in alignment. The more removed we are from our authentic self, the more likely we are to suffer from poor mental health and experience an unease with life.

As you may have guessed, I don't have much patience for all those "enlightened" gurus and so now that they've grabbed ownership of the word 'authenticity', I'm a little hesitant to use it. But I'd like to ask you to ignore all the fluff and just focus on the fact that authenticity is key to true happiness.

## What is authenticity?

You may know authenticity as the voice that speaks to you in those quiet moments but you don't really listen to. You may even know authenticity by another name – intuition – which, again, we rarely take much notice of.

Author and world peace advocate Norman Cousins proclaimed that "the tragedy of life is not death but what we let die inside of us while we live".

If there's one thing, I'd love you to leave with when you put this book down it is to understand the enormity of that quote and then to make a promise to yourself that you will start living your life on your terms.

Before we continue I'm going to invite you to do the following reflection. You'll need your workbook which, if you haven't already, you can download from my website, annazannides.com.

Okay, ready?

**Reflection on authenticity**

Find a quiet space, one that feels safe to you, and make yourself comfortable. I'd recommend switching off all distractions and noise – yes, even your phone.

Remember in the previous reflection, on page 40, I explained that when you do a reflective practice, you shouldn't try hard to find an answer; you should be in a relaxed state and allow whatever presents itself to rise to the surface. Or if you need further support with this, pop over to my website, annazannides.com, for ways you can get my personal support.

Start by taking a nice, slow breath and then write out the first question from the following list. Take as much time as you need to reflect on the question and then write whatever comes to mind. Don't judge it or try to edit it – just write (or draw or even record yourself speaking).

1. Answer the following questions:
   a. What are the main points that have resonated with you so far from reading this book? (Please be honest. If nothing has, then write "nothing.")
   b. Has anything come up for you in response to what you have read and if yes, what?
   c. Have any memories resurfaced and if so, are you surprised by them?
   d. Has any significant childhood event sprung to mind from what you have read so far?
2. Spend some time reflecting on this question: **what do I want?**

   Just write whatever comes to mind – no filter. We'll come back to this at the end of the book and check if there's been any changes. For now, just write it and forget about it.

## Section summary

### Key points:

- We looked at the science behind our social conditioning and how that leads to us disconnecting from our authentic self.

- Not being ourselves in no way implies that we are fake or even that every part of our life conflicts with our true values.
- It is quite possible that you are in a healthy, loving relationship but that your working life is causing you unhappiness. Or it could be that you're feeling less connected to your partner because you aren't heading in the same direction.
- You don't need to be falling apart to want to align your life with your true values and purpose; however, if it feels like your whole life is out of sync, then this is a great place to start.

In the next part of the book, we'll explore how social norms and the narrative of the linear life plays out in your life. You will be challenged to look at your life in a deeper way than you may be used to because I want to help you see where you are stuck and why.

## PART TWO
## THIS IS HOW YOU GOT HERE

Social norms are the informal, unwritten rules that define what is acceptable and appropriate in our society. We could say they act as our moral code to help society to function so we can live together in relative harmony. However, when these social norms infringe on our individuality, they become questionable. And as we all know, life is never a level playing field. Some are born with the advantages that many can only dream of. So is there a more sinister reason behind some of these social norms, and do they serve to keep us from pursuing our individual aspirations?

In one of his talks, the philosopher Krishnamurti said, "It is no measure of health to be well adjusted to a profoundly sick society." What this means is that you are able to go along with the programme; you are able to study hard and do well at school. You play by the rules and you are okay with that. And that is perfectly fine if you agree with the system and believe it is a good one.

It's also okay if you believe that the direction this system is taking you in is where you want to go. However, for many of us, it has become harder to believe we are living in the right world and this can often lead to us thinking that we are the problem, rather than the problem being the society we live in.

I would like to challenge the notion that there is something inherently wrong with us and instead urge you to consider the possibility that the programme we have been conditioned to follow may be flawed. This programme was designed for us, and we have consistently adjusted our behaviour to conform to it. It is worth noting that the current media focus on mental health has created a lucrative industry that thrives on making us feel as though we are not quite right. However, instead of simply addressing the symptoms of mental health issues, we must examine the root causes of these problems. While I acknowledge that mental health concerns are real and important, the current approach to addressing them may not be effective.

The primary objective of this book is to reshape the narrative and prompt you to critically assess the harmful aspects of society while acknowledging its positive elements. Instead of unquestioningly accepting these negative attributes, this book aims to help you question the narratives you have adopted and take control of your own life.

The system we live in places a strong emphasis on our relationships with others, which includes a flawed and potentially unhealthy definition of love. Given the significant amount of time we devote to seeking love, it is a fitting starting point for the next section of the book.

## Love and Relationships

Shortly after my divorce, I started dating again. And I can tell you, it wasn't easy to get back out there after being married for three decades. Not only because I'd been with the same man since the age of twenty-two but also because, back then, there was only one way to meet someone and that was in person. There was no such thing as online dating back then; in fact, there was no such thing as online, full stop! If someone had told me that one day people would download an app (a what???) and then start flicking through random photos on a phone in the hope they would meet their next big love, I'd have told them they'd been watching too much *Star Trek*. And yet here I was at fifty-two doing just that.

Even though at the beginning of my marriage breakdown life was tough and I was pretty much broken, it wasn't long after that I suddenly found a new zest for life. There was nobody waiting for me when I got home anymore because I'd sold the house and rented my first bachelorette apartment. My kids were grown up and my ex-husband was truly out of my life. Suddenly I was able to ask, "Anna, what do *you* want?" And it felt good. No, I lie – it felt great!

So, I started looking after myself. I hired a personal trainer, and we'd train together almost every day. I hadn't given myself that sort of attention for decades and I loved every minute that I now had to spoil myself. My ex-husband used to eye up every woman who came into his view and although at the beginning we'd fight about it, later I just stopped caring. However, I didn't realise until I was single how much that had affected my self-confidence. I really didn't believe any man would find me attractive.

It was a friend who set up my online profile on a dating site for the first time and who helped me navigate my new single world. And it wasn't long after that I started dating again. Well, dating might be a slight misnomer because I'm not sure those apps should be called dating sites at all. I could probably write a book on my experiences but that's not the point of this book and it's already been done so many times. And I rather like my privacy.

Anyway, one day I agreed to meet a rather handsome, well-dressed man in a café after we had been chatting online for a while. *Ha*, I thought, *not bad*.

He was polite, bought me a coffee and we got chatting. It turned out that he was married. It's not unusual to find married people on these dating apps. He explained he had a successful career, a lovely house and owned a couple of luxury cars. He found my disinterest in his materialistic view a little strange. I asked him why he was on a dating site and if it was his first time, to which he replied, "I have a good marriage. It's just that my wife doesn't give me sex as much as I want."

And no, it wasn't his first time. In fact, he'd had several sexual encounters throughout his very happy marriage. He blamed his wife for his "need" to have sex with other women. Of course, a good sexual relationship is important in a marriage but to think your relationship is happy while you are out trying to score has got to be hypocrisy.

As we talked, his insistence that his marriage was both happy and healthy strengthened as he went on to explain that the extramarital sexual encounters were his way of letting off steam and de-stressing from work pressures. Even after I told him I teach mindfulness and that might help, he stayed true to his intention: sex was his de-stresser!

As far as he was concerned, his marriage was working. And it was for him, because he was doing as he pleased. He had a great career, a beautiful home, a good lifestyle and a loving wife but there is a fundamental flaw with his perspective. His wife was living a different life, one where she was married to a devoted man whom she could trust; when he was "working late", she was dutifully preparing his dinner. Of course, there was always the possibility that deep down she knew but I have a sneaky suspicion she had no idea. Who really knows what goes on in other people's lives and in their relationships?

I've included this story to emphasise a crucial point: in any relationship, we are limited by our own perceptions and perspectives, making it impossible to truly know the other person. For instance, the wife in this story may have held the belief that she was married to a trustworthy, hardworking and devoted husband.

In contrast, the husband had convinced himself he wasn't engaging in any wrongdoing and that sex was unrelated to love. However, a closer examination reveals he was using sex as a means of escaping the monotony of his life. Meanwhile, his wife was in love, or at least believed she was in a loving relationship, with someone who existed only in her own perception.

I want to make it clear that I don't intend to pass judgement since relationships are complex, and as you will see later in this book, the notion of monogamy and traditional relationships are part of our social constructs. If all parties involved were consenting adults of sound mind and had agreed to it, there would be nothing inherently wrong with either of them having extramarital sex.

Many of us seek romantic relationships because we believe another person can make us feel happy, or because we are afraid of being alone. In the scenario described above, it is possible that both the husband and wife were fulfilling their needs. The wife may have grown so accustomed to the security and comforts of her marriage that she was content in her blissful ignorance. However, I cannot help but wonder what would have happened if she had discovered her husband's true nature. Would her perception of him have changed?

From my personal experience, I think the answer is probably yes.

You see, up to the point when I received the text on the day my marriage ended, I had the belief that my husband was the one person I could always rely on – that whatever happened he'd have my back and despite some of the things I didn't like about him, I never believed he was anything but a devoted husband and father. However, in the instant that I read the text everything changed. It was like the man I'd known for over thirty years had disappeared and standing in front of me was a stranger.

In that split second, my whole view of my relationship and my life changed. Because when we step out of the story we hold in our mind and see it from a different perspective, especially if we are forced to see things with new information, our whole reality shifts. This isn't some sort of emotional viewpoint; it is scientific. You may have heard the saying 'once seen, it cannot be unseen'; this explains the simple fact that every situation can only be interpreted based on the information we have at the time. And when new information is presented to us, suddenly it's like we are seeing the same person or situation with different eyes. We covered this earlier when we looked at perspective and this is just one example of how our perspective changes when we find out something new or different.

Society has created an unhealthy view of love, confusing it with attachment, desire and dependency. When we look at someone from the view of 'what can they do for me?', we are trying to fill a gap in our own world and fulfilling a self-serving need.

Love should bring us joy, yet often it is the greatest source of our sorrows because when it doesn't work out, it can be devastating. Bessel van der Kolk writes, "The most human suffering is related to love and loss."

But is it that love is the problem, or that we don't really understand love?

## What is love?

The *Oxford English Dictionary* defines love as "a very strong feeling of liking and caring for somebody/something, especially a member of your family or a friend. Romantic love includes sexual intimacy."

In Buddhism, true love is called *maitri* or *metta* and is quite different from the love described above.

Love from a Buddhist perspective comes with no strings attached and it does not depend on mutual adoration or that our personal needs are met or even that our partner fulfils our sexual urges. Love for our children does not depend on them pleasing us or living according to our standards or wishes. In Buddhism, love for our children is pure in that all we want is for them to be happy. The rest is their choice.

Ancient Greek philosophers distinguished between three types of love: *eros*, *agape* and *philia*. *Eros* is a kind of passionate desire for an object, typically sexual passion. This type of love is described as egocentric love; its main purpose is to satisfy our own desires and can be seen as a selfish type of love. *Agape* is the sort of love we have for each other, like a brotherly or sisterly love.

This love is often spontaneous and unmotivated. And *philia* is more like affection – the type of feelings you have for a friend. In fact, *philia* comes from the word for friend in Greek.

In Hinduism, love is broken down into five stages, starting with what is called *Kama*. This stage of love is sensory craving, what we commonly call physical attraction. This is what the ancient Greeks called *eros*, simply erotic sex. This type of love is purely to satisfy a personal desire and as such the joy is short-lived. Unlike Judeo-Christian beliefs, this sort of love is not seen as something to be ashamed of or a sin but more as a joyous aspect of human existence. However, it is described as fleeting. In other words, when it ends, we can be left feeling empty and end up chasing the next experience to feel good again.

The next stage is called *Shringara*, which also involves desire and sexual pleasure. However, unlike *Kama*, *Shringara* includes emotional intimacy – there is more personal connection and it can be more fulfilling. The third stage of love is *Maitri*, defined as generous compassion. This kind of love is much closer to what is described in theological texts, the sort of love we are all capable of – like the love a mother has for a child. We express this love through kindness to others, even to strangers, and it often has no personal motive other than to be kind.

The fourth stage of love in Hinduism is called *Bhakti*, which is described as impersonal devotion. It is personified in people such as Nelson Mandela, Martin

Luther King, Florence Nightingale and countless others whose love for the world was more powerful than any singular romance – their love was for the greater good and impacted thousands of lives for the better.

And the final stage is *Atma-Prema*, translated as unconditional self-love. Up to this point, all the stages of love have been pointed outwards, but by this stage we understand that we are not separate from others. Rather, we begin to see ourselves in others and see others in ourselves. As the Indian Sufi poet Kabir said, "The river that flows in you also flows in me." When we reach this stage, we recognise that when we strip away all the labels of heritage and upbringing, we understand how we are all essentially one. At this point, our love loses its boundaries and becomes unconditional. As the wise poet Rumi wrote:

*I, you, he, she, we –*
*In the garden of mystic lovers,*
*these are not true distinctions.*

Buddhism teaches that all love relies on self-love. If we do not understand our own innate goodness, if we cannot offer self-kindness, then we cannot offer real love to others. In 1990, Sharon Salzberg, author and one of America's leading spiritual teachers, attended a small conference in India. Here, she was given the opportunity to ask the Dalai Lama a question. In her book *Loving Kindness*, she states that at the time she was in a bad place, full of self-loathing and negative self-thinking. So she asked:

"Your Holiness, what do you think about self-hatred?"

Salzberg goes on to say that the Dalai Lama looked "somewhat confused" and replied, "What's self-hatred?" He genuinely had no idea what she was asking, so Salzberg went on to explain what self-hatred meant. To which the Dalai Lama responded, "How could you think of yourself that way?"

This conversation highlights an underlying belief in our culture that self-love is a form of selfishness, which contrasts with the Buddhist perspective, especially the Tibetan Buddhist view that all love depends on our capacity to offer self-love. It starts with the premise that unless we truly understand the preciousness of our own life and the privilege of being born a human with the opportunities that this gives us, then we cannot truly understand love and compassion. What the Dalai Lama was trying to demonstrate is that if you are self-loathing and critical of yourself, you lower your capacity to give and accept love.

In basic terms, this could mean that if your inner world is full of anger, resentment, hate and a view that the world is a bad place, then this is what you project out into the world. It also means that whenever you engage with others, there is an element of self-gain – even when you love, you expect to get something in return. The question then is: is that real love?

I like to explain it like this: if I stop to let someone cross the road and they don't say thank you or acknowledge my good deed, do I get offended? If I do, then was my intention genuine, or was it to gain some sort of recognition for being kind? I'm not saying we shouldn't thank someone who is kind to us; however, if that is our motivation, then it is coming from a self-indulgent desire. The same applies with love. If we give love with an expectation to get something in return, then is that really love, or our need to be loved?

If we look at these different views about love, we may understand why it is so easy to fall in and out of love. We are only in love as long as our object of love is fulfilling our desires and as long as they are making us feel good about ourselves. Yogi Sadhguru describes our interpretation of love as "a sort of friends with benefits". And he has a point, if we aren't getting some sort of benefit, then we are no longer in love.

Of course, this is a very idealistic way to look at love. It is virtually impossible to have unconditional love for anyone, except perhaps for your children. Nor is it advisable to be in love with someone who is bad for you. That can't be real love in any case.

It is, however, both useful and important to reflect on our personal interpretation of love and how that affects how we relate to others.

> **Reflection on love**
>
> I'd like to invite you to take a bit of time to reflect on the following questions before you continue. You may want to reach for your workbook so you can write your answers.
>
> - Is my view of love derived from my cultural upbringing?
> - What would I have been like if I had been born somewhere else and at a different time?
> - When I love, what do I expect in return?
>
> The purpose of this reflection is to start challenging your views on love and relationships – to dig deep into those ingrained beliefs about how to love, who to love and to identify repeating patterns in your relationships.
>
> When you feel you've given yourself enough time to think about these questions, put your notes aside so we can continue to look at relationships.

## Relationships

In her book *The Truth Will Set You Free, But First It Will Piss You Off!*, Gloria Steinem writes: "Only after I saw women who were attracted to distant, condescending, even violent men did I begin to understand that having a distant, condescending, even violent father could make those qualities seem inevitable, even feel like home. Because of my father, only kindness felt like home."

Looking at relationships from this perspective has helped me understand why I appeared to be drawn to emotionally immature and narcissistic men: it was familiar to me. My father was someone who not only fitted Steinem's description of being "distant", but he was also an addict. Often, addicts struggle with low self-esteem and may have difficulty forming healthy relationships as their main priority is getting their next high, regardless of the consequences.

It's common for individuals to develop patterns in their relationships, and in my case I observed another recurring theme – a tendency to compensate for my partners' lack of intellectual depth by downplaying my own intelligence. This behaviour may have stemmed from a desire to connect with my partners on a deeper level, or perhaps a fear of intimidating them with my intellect. However, over time, I realised this approach was not fulfilling and often resulted in unbalanced and unsatisfying relationships.

I came to understand that a healthy relationship is based on mutual respect, honesty and open communication. In order to form a fulfilling and meaningful connection with your partner, it's essential to be true to yourself and not compromise your values or intelligence to please someone else. It's important to acknowledge that both men and women can have a significant influence on their attitudes and behaviours in relationships. In my case, I recognised that my mother, and other women of her generation, served as role models for me, and their behaviour may have shaped my own approach to relationships.

I observed that many women of my mother's generation often acted as pleasers, and sometimes used their sexuality to get what they wanted in relationships. While this behaviour may have been a survival strategy for them at the time, it may have also reinforced certain unhealthy patterns that can carry over into future generations.

It's understandable that our childhood experiences and family dynamics can greatly influence our attitudes and behaviours in relationships, often leading us to misunderstand and even get love and relationships wrong. It's important to recognise that relationships are complex and individualised and can be heavily influenced by our personal needs and interpretations.

Additionally, the societal narratives around love, relationships and sex can be confusing and often lead to unrealistic expectations. You may not know how to relate to others in a healthy and fulfilling way because you were bombarded with messages about what love and relationships should look like, without taking into account your own unique experiences and perspectives.

It's crucial that you become aware of these influences and actively work to overcome them. By developing self-awareness and exploring your own values and needs in relationships, you can develop more fulfilling connections with others based on mutual respect, communication and understanding.

This is something we explore in the final part of this book but for now let's look at why relationships are challenging.

In 2021, the average divorce rate in the UK was 42%, representing a slight decrease from the previous years. The most common divorce age is between 40 and 44, with an average of 62% of divorces filed by women.

Although it might at first appear that the divorce rate is falling, these statistics don't take into consideration the rise in people who are cohabiting and, therefore, don't form part of the data.

In 2020, the Divorce, Dissolution and Separation Act came into effect in the UK. This new law introduced the 'no-fault' divorce, meaning that divorce is much easier today and less costly. And did you know that divorce lawyers have peak seasons? Typically, these are September and January every year. The reason divorce spikes at these times is because they follow long holiday periods or are seen as new beginnings – the start of the new school year and new calendar year.

It is near impossible to measure how many relationships break down, because we don't hold that sort of information. And of course, there are many people in loving, caring relationships, so let's not forget that.

## Unpacking the social narrative on relationships

Our beliefs are formed from a young age and are mostly influenced by the collective storylines we grow up hearing. These come together to create our personal narrative, and influence what we believe about ourselves.

For example, you may believe you are good at art, but where did that idea come from?

You may very well be good at art; however, if this was confirmed by an adult in your younger years, you are more likely to accept it as true. Just like if someone tells you that you are beautiful as a child, you will grow up believing you are. However, if you were told as a child that you aren't creative, or nobody ever looked at you and said, "Wow! You are beautiful," then you won't believe it as you grow up. If you add to that what we covered previously about inheriting behaviours and belief systems through our ancestors, then it is obvious that your self-belief is not a reflection of who you really are but who you think you are.

Family stories that are retold often become ingrained in our identities, shaping the character of our family as a whole. Sometimes we don't know how they affect us until something happens in our life and we look to make some sense out of it. In my case it was when my marriage ended that I started to explore the theme of divorce in my family, which dated back to the early 1900s with my great-grandmother.

## My great-grandmother

When I was around five or six my sister and I were sent to Cyprus to stay with our maternal grandparents for a couple of months. I assume it was so that my parents could work without having to worry about us. My grandfather was a cobbler, with a small but busy workshop in the heart of the capital, Nicosia. The centre of the city was wrapped around the open-air market. Every morning, people from the surrounding villages would set up their stands to sell their fresh produce. An array of colours would line the cobbled stones, the best fruit and vegetables on display. It was a bustling, crowded place and yet people seemed to know each other.

On the street corner opposite my grandfather's shop was a room; the door was usually open so you could see the dark, almost-bare space inside. In that room lay an elderly lady, on a big metal-frame bed. Her white hair tied up and covered with a black net to keep it flat. The woman was my great-grandmother and sometimes I'd walk over to see her. These are the only memories I have of her, but her story was often told in our family, and it goes something like this:

Cyprus in the late 1800s was largely agricultural and, like many places in the world at the time, women had limited freedom, so life was especially harsh for them. However, despite those limitations, my great-grandmother divorced her husband and even managed to gain sole custody of her only daughter – something quite unheard of at the time.

Although her husband was a drunk, she had to fight for custody of her daughter because in those days men were automatically given custody. Fearing she would lose her daughter, my great-grandmother decided to tell the judge that she didn't know who the real father of her daughter was. In the absence of DNA tests, the judge was forced to decide in favour of my great-grandmother, awarding her full custody. It is also said that she was a woman who commanded respect from others, so we also believe the judge knew that although my great-grandmother had lied, it was the right thing to do.

Her life was difficult. A woman raising a child alone in a society that ostracised divorced women could not have been easy. To survive, she worked nights, washing sheets by hand. The story goes that as she walked home after her shifts, men would try to force themselves on her. In those days any woman who dared to divorce her husband would be seen as stained. To protect herself, she carried a knife, hidden in a garter under her dress, and when she needed to, threatened to use it. This soon became common knowledge and men learned to leave her alone. I've always found my great-grandmother's story fascinating; it taught me that women are more than capable of looking after themselves.

Decades later, my mother divorced my father after twenty-two years of marriage. My father was a gambling addict, which meant he was often absent, and mostly unreliable. By the age of twenty-two my mother had three children and was trapped in a dysfunctional relationship, living thousands of miles from her family.

Eventually, she filed for divorce. However, even though my mother was in London, which was far more progressive than Cyprus at the time, divorce was still stigmatised, especially in our tight-knit community. She had attempted to leave my father several times during their marriage, but her parents would not accept the shame of having a divorced daughter with three children. Each time my mother flew to Cyprus to beg to stay, explaining how difficult her life was in England, her parents would give her money and send her back to her husband. I remember a couple of years before my parents' divorce hearing my grandfather tell my mother: "While I am alive, you will never leave your husband." I wonder if it was a coincidence or a conscious decision for my mother to divorce only after her father died.

The story I shared above gave me the perspective that women don't need to stay in unhappy relationships. Having these women in my life also showed me that women do not have to be meek or even looked after. On the other hand, I also grew up with many stories that reflected negatively on men – 'they are always unreliable' was the underlying theme.

Growing up surrounded by women who had to be strong and an emotionally absent father meant that I too became the 'strong one'. And while that is in many ways a compliment, it also means that you are the one that people expect will just get on with it. So, in the end you do just that – you become so self-sufficient that you rarely allow others into your nice, safe world.

I can see how all this links to me and how that story has played out in my own life. Now it's time to look at the stories in your life that may have impacted you in your relationships.

Let's take a little break – time to reach for your notebook.

> **Reflection on relationships: part one**
>
> By now you should be familiar with these reflection parts of the book but just in case you need a little reminder, take yourself to that quiet place and sit comfortably. And when you are ready, do the following:
>
> - Start paying attention to whatever is floating in your mind. See if you can just sit with it, without getting too involved. Now, when you are ready, open your notebook and just write whatever comes to you, based on what you read in the previous section.
>
> - Then, draw a line under the previous task and answer the following questions:
>   - What story dominates my family character?
>   - How does that continue in my own life?
>
> Take as long as you need to answer these questions and to reflect.

## Section summary

### Key points:

- Your perspective on relationships and those you chose to be in relationships with are mostly driven by your childhood experiences.
- It is important to acknowledge that your behaviour and attitudes play a part in how your relationships work – blaming your partner isn't useful for either of you.
- The stories that are repeated in your family are the stories that form the character of your family.
- You don't just get your image of men from your father or father figure; you also get it from your mother. Therefore, to understand why you have certain beliefs about men or women, you should explore how you experienced both as you were growing up.

The final point leads nicely into the upcoming chapter, which explores how our gender roles impact our behaviour in romantic relationships.

## Gender Roles

Margaret Atwood famously said, "Men are afraid that women will laugh at them. Women are afraid that men will kill them." A hauntingly accurate statement that speaks volumes about the deeply ingrained fears and expectations we face as we navigate our gendered existence.

As a young girl, I defied societal norms by choosing to play football with the boys instead of playing with dolls. I shunned dresses and makeup, preferring the comfort of jeans, T-shirts and trainers. My choices left my mother perplexed and others questioning my sexuality.

But why must we be confined to narrow definitions of femininity and masculinity?

Why can't we just be who we are, without fear of judgement or violence?

Well let's unpack that question a little bit.

### The fairy tales

When my twin granddaughters were around seven years old, realising they had reached that critical stage in their development, I decided to conduct a little experiment to find out what they were thinking.

To kick off the conversation, I asked them about their favourite stories.

"Sofia, how does *Frozen* end?"

"Which one, *Yiayia*?" (Note: *Yiayia* is Granny in Greek).

"Any one you want," I replied.

"In *Frozen 2* Anna marries Kristoff," Sofia replied with that beautiful innocence I love so much in children.

"Ah, do you think that's a happy ending?" I asked her.

"Yes!" she said with her familiar cheeky smile.

I turned to Olivia.

"Olivia, I know you love Belle in *Beauty and the Beast*. How does her story end?"

"She marries the Beast, and they live happily ever after," she responded in a matter-of-fact manner.

As we chatted further, my granddaughters eagerly shared their love for classic fairy tales like *Sleeping Beauty* and *Cinderella*. I couldn't help but wonder how these stories were moulding their young minds. Would they internalise the messages of these tales, or would they just be fleeting moments of entertainment? As we know, repeated exposure to certain narratives can deeply influence our values and beliefs.

Only time will tell how these stories will shape their views on life. However, if they continue to be repeated over and over, it's safe to assume they will play a significant role in defining their perspectives.

The myth of 'living happily ever after' holds significant power and can shape the self-perception of both boys and girls. Following the "interview" with my granddaughters, I conducted further research and came across the work of Colette Dowling. In her book *The Cinderella Complex: Women's Hidden Fear of Independence*, Dowling describes a genuine psychological phenomenon known as the Cinderella complex. This condition is characterised by a woman's fear of true independence and a subconscious expectation that a 'knight in shining armour' will rescue and provide for her.

You may be wondering, what's wrong with the idea of a knight in shining armour coming to our rescue? My question is, what's right about it? Our lives are precious, and we should take ownership of them instead of waiting for someone to take care of us. And at the very least, we should know how to take care of ourselves.

As Bob Dylan wisely said, "If you're not busy being born, you're busy dying."

The fairy tales we often encounter may appear benign, but their underlying themes can have a powerful and long-lasting influence on us, often without our conscious awareness. Consider *Cinderella*, for instance, in which the prince only acknowledges her *after* she puts on the missing glass slipper, despite having previously met her at the ball. Does this imply that we're only visible and valuable when we're dressed up and prettified? Similarly, in *Beauty and the Beast*, Belle manages to domesticate an enraged and deformed creature with her physical attractiveness. Despite the Beast's initial hostile demeanour, she still ends up falling in love with him.

The implicit messages that both boys and girls are exposed to from infancy play a pivotal role in shaping our socialisation and personality development. The idea of a female protagonist who requires a male saviour, and a male character who must assume the role of the hero to save the day, is a common motif in fairy tales. It's probably no coincidence that most fairy tales are written by men. What happens when reality fails to align with these stories? More significantly, how do our childhood impressions and beliefs impact our capacity to establish meaningful adult relationships that are healthy and satisfying?

When our unaddressed childhood traumas and those passed down from our ancestors continue to influence our lives as adults, it can be extremely difficult to build healthy relationships, let alone ones that mirror the fairy tales we were exposed to in our formative years.

The following story illustrates how my difficulties with trust were shaped. I hope it might prompt you to reflect on your own experiences and identify the root causes of your own feelings of insecurity.

## Lost trust

> *"Don't expect the person that hurts you to be the person that saves you."*
> – unknown

It was a regular Sunday and our family of five were all at home. I am a middle child with a sister who is three years older and a brother who is two years younger. At the time of this event, I was around nine but possibly a little younger.

My brother and I were peacefully playing with his Matchbox cars on his cosy bedroom floor, and my sister was listening to music in our bedroom, when suddenly our parents' yelling disrupted our tranquillity. I had become accustomed to their arguments as a normal part of life, but I noticed that my brother seemed frightened. So, to try to comfort him I told him to keep playing and to ignore our parents. I attempted to distract him, hoping the commotion would soon end. However, their shouting only grew louder, and so we began to speak louder to drown out the noise. Suddenly we were startled by my mother calling out for help, followed by our father calling us downstairs to see "your stupid mother!" Without hesitation, the three of us bolted downstairs to find my father sitting on top of my mother, with his hands around her neck.

My father wasn't usually a violent man. His bark was louder than his bite; however, he had an awful mouth, especially towards my mother. He often degraded her in front of us and I believe she became resilient to the verbal abuse. And although my mother was rather fearless, on that day even I could see she was scared. So, without warning, the three of us leaped onto my father, shouting, "Leave her alone," while trying to pull him off our mother.

Then he suddenly turned to face me, picked me up, opened the front door and placed me outside.

And he began to express how disappointed he was in me.

As I stood looking up at my father, a tall and formidable figure whose imposing shadow engulfed my small frame, I felt like crying but there was a part of me that refused to show weakness, even back then. Still a young child, I lacked the ability to articulate my feelings, so I remained frozen while I watched him slam the door shut, leaving me standing outside alone. In that moment, any trust I had for my father was shattered. For the rest of his life, I maintained a distance from him, which only grew stronger as I got older.

Not only did he never attempt to bridge that gap but he later blamed me for my mother's decision to divorce him. In his view, it was my support that gave her the courage to leave. He may have had a point. Maybe I did give my mother the strength to finally end her marriage, but that's a huge burden to put on a young girl. What made it worse was that whenever I tried to talk to my family about this incident, and others like it, I was told to not exaggerate or be unfair on my father. Eventually

I started to believe that perhaps I was the problem after all, because nobody else seemed to see it the way I did.

It wasn't until I started working with a counsellor in my early fifties that I realised the extent of the damage caused by that incident.

As I recounted the event to my therapist, I didn't expect much given my past experiences. However, when I'd finished, my therapist looked at me and declared, "That was abuse, Anna."

For the first time, I felt heard and validated. My voice mattered. We continued our discussions over the following weeks, delving into the complexities of my relationship with my father. I revealed how his gambling addiction had consumed our family life. Sometimes, he would vanish for days without checking in, leaving my mother to shoulder the responsibilities alone. On good days, he would return with his winnings, rousing us from our slumber and doling out cash. However, on bad days, when he lost everything, he would head straight to bed and sleep for an entire day, avoiding the world.

The days when my father was at home were different, particularly when my mother was absent. She was the axis around which our lives revolved. When she was away, pursuing her own interests, I would shut myself in my room, avoiding any interaction with my father.

My father's gambling addiction often caused intense arguments between my parents, especially as my mother became more assertive and less tolerant. We went through many tough times as a family, including the day when the bank locked us out of our own house because the mortgage hadn't been paid. That day, my mother had to break a window to get us back in. She eventually managed to negotiate with the bank and saved our home.

Our house looked onto a park where my friends and I spent a lot of time playing. One day, while we were playing football, one of the boys asked me what was happening at my house. So I turned to look back at our house to see my mother throwing things into the garden while my father sat passively, playing the victim. I felt embarrassed and tried to play it off as a joke, but the situation was far from funny.

During our sessions, my therapist asked me why I downplayed the severity of what had happened in my family. This made me realise I had internalised the belief that I didn't have the right to be angry with my father, and that I somehow shared the blame for his inability to show me love.

In my narrative, I depict how the inequalities between men and women had a significant impact, particularly during my parents' era, when women had limited rights and opportunities, compelling them to remain in unfulfilling relationships. Moreover, my assumption of responsibility for my father's emotional shortcomings is a by-product of a society that has historically allowed men to escape accountability for their actions.

It is worth noting that although society has made strides in recent times, gender inequality still persists. While expectations for girls and boys are slowly becoming more balanced, there is still a long way to go. Despite progress, domestic abuse remains a severe issue, with women at a higher risk of being murdered by their partner than a stranger. Additionally, children are more likely to experience abuse from a parent than a stranger.

It is important not to compare your childhood with mine. That isn't why I've shared it with you. What is important is that regardless of whether your experience of trauma was worse than mine or less severe, it's important to give it the acknowledgement it deserves. Your personal experience is valid and worthy of recognition because it is part of who you are today.

So let's explore how your past might be showing up in your present life.

## Playing out our past

Romantic relationships are not just made up of two individuals; they also include all the past histories and experiences of each person. We might call that 'baggage' and contrary to what we may think, we all have it. Some may have a lighter load and others might have trunks full; nevertheless, none of us go into relationships, not even friendships, without our 'stuff'.

In my case, my strained relationship with my father resulted in a tendency to mistrust and hold back in relationships, which was made worse by being married to a man who believed men had the right to eye up any woman who passed by. He would openly flirt with other women in front of me, yet would become possessive if another man showed interest in me. Without a clear understanding of what makes a healthy relationship, I mistook this behaviour as love or normal.

Not long after the birth of my first son, my neighbour knocked on the front door while I was alone at home. He asked to come inside as he had something important to tell me. I felt comfortable enough to let him in, as his wife was a good friend and the four of us had become close too. I invited him into our front room and we both sat down. Then he declared that my husband and his wife were having an affair, and that everyone except us knew about it.

I had grown accustomed to my husband's flirtatious behaviour, and although at times it really did upset me, I ended up believing it was just his way. In this case I also found it difficult to believe that my friend, who I'd grown close to, would betray me. I was well aware of the problems in their marriage, so I decided to take his story with a pinch of salt. But I was angry because my husband's disregard for women was fuelling my lack of trust and making me even more insecure than I was before my marriage. When I asked him about it, he was dismissive and even suggested the problem wasn't him but me. When my father found out, instead of confronting his son-in-law, he calmly looked at me and asked, "What did you do wrong?"

Following this episode, I left with my son and went to Cyprus to stay with my mother, who had remarried. Although I returned home after a few weeks, having discussed the situation with my husband, our marriage never quite recovered. Something inside me had changed. Despite this, I stayed with him because there was a part of me that believed I was the problem. Well, when your father tells you it's you and your husband confirms it, then surely it's got to be you.

Ten years later, despite having three young children, a similar event happened. Initially, I gave him the benefit of the doubt, as that's what we're supposed to do, right? However, this time it wasn't just about me, but also our children. I couldn't imagine raising them alone and knew they needed their father, even if I wasn't happy with him as a husband. But instead of blindly trusting him again, I made a decision for myself. I decided to focus on establishing a career and vowed to be in a position to take care of my children and myself if something like this were to happen again. So I went to university, earned the degree I should have achieved years ago and built a successful career. As the main earner, we decided that I would focus on my career while he took on the childcaring role, even though the children were now in school. This arrangement worked, improving our financial situation and allowing me to escape the monotony of our relationship. I encouraged him to pursue his own interests, perhaps retrain for a more enjoyable career, but he didn't seem interested. Our differences became apparent, with me always striving for self-improvement while he seemed to believe he was perfect as he was.

When I received the text that ended our marriage, I knew deep down that it was inevitable and had been a long time coming. I had little doubt that the period of compromise had come to an end and it was time for me to live my life.

A few years after my divorce, I was introduced to the teachings of Milarepa. Jetsun Milarepa was a Tibetan *siddha* (Sanskrit for 'The Perfect One' or 'one who is accomplished'). He was famously known as a murderer when he was a young man, before turning to the teachings of the Buddha. He later became a highly accomplished disciple of the Buddha and is famous for his songs and poems. When I first heard this one, it resonated with me deeply:

*When you look at your lover, first your lover is a smiling goddess. Later she is a vicious woman. Finally, she is a black-faced demoness. Desire for a lover is disastrous.*

When reading this text, keep in mind that it was written in the early 11th century so the words might sound harsh and outdated; however, it simply refers to impermanence – that everything changes. This teaching also touches on another key Buddhist teaching: attachment. These two teachings form a huge part of the *dharma* and give us a contrasting view of life to the one we learn in contemporary society. By *dharma* I am referring to the teachings of the Buddha, although it can also mean the nature of reality in Buddhism.

As I worked through my divorce and began to put my life back together, I found these teachings gave me clarity. To keep in mind that nothing stays the same and that everything is changing, including ourselves and the people we love, means we should never be attached to anything. I'm not saying we should become detached and uncaring. What we must do is understand that when we put all our hopes into one relationship, we are resting a huge part of our happiness on one aspect of life. When my marriage came to an end, I came to see that it wasn't heartbreak I was dealing with – in fact, I doubt love had much to do with it. What I was facing was my attachment to the story of 'happily ever after'.

To fully understand this term 'attachment' and to gain some insights into why so many relationships end badly, or end at all, I started to research the subject. And now single for the first time in three decades, there was a lot to learn. I needed to make sense of it all because thirty years is a long time to be with someone and end up not knowing them and, what's worse, not knowing yourself.

Before we start to explore attachment and how it may affect your life today, let's stop to reflect on what we've covered in the previous few pages.

> **Reflection on gender roles**
>
> I'm aware some of what we've covered above might be heavy, so I'm going to ask you to just sit with it. I'd suggest a bit of time to focus on your breath and, if need be, give yourself a little self-kindness.
>
> You can find a guided meditation for this on my website, annazannides.com, or do the following:
>
> Sit or lie down somewhere comfortable. Take a few soft, slow breaths, in through your nose and out through your nose. Give your body some time to settle into the quiet space. Then put your hand on your heart and repeat a mantra that feels soothing for you. It could be something like "I am well, I am safe and I am at ease." Repeat until you are ready to let it go.

You may not be familiar with this type of breathing meditation as it is commonly thought that you should breathe in through your nose and out through your mouth. There is a reason we practise mindful breathing in this way. The guided meditations on my website may help you with this if you find it difficult or need help.

Now let's explore attachment a little more so you can gain a better understanding of how it plays out in your life.

## Attachment

In their book, *Attached: The New Science of Adult Attachment*, Amir Levine and Rachel Heller argue that dependency and attachment theory is "based on the assertion that the need to be in a close relationship is embedded in our genes" and to support their argument they refer to the work of John Bowlby who we met in Part One.

Bowlby was a British psychologist, born in the early 1900s, and was best known for his work in child development. He pioneered what came to be known as attachment theory and concluded that "we've been programmed by evolution to single out a few specific individuals in our lives and make them precious to us".

The idea that we are programmed and predetermined by our genes was something I discussed in Part One when we looked at the different perspectives provided through new sciences such as epigenetics, quantum physics and neuroscience. Of course, a child needs to be loved and cared for to become a healthy adult. Remember Maslow's hierarchy of needs? However, attachment theory seems to imply that we are confined and even fated by our early life, even trapped by the relationship we had with our mother. But we are evolving creatures – is it possible that our first few months or possibly early years predetermine our whole life? Personally, I think this science is a little outdated and while useful because it gives us some understanding of early childhood behaviour, it can also form a type of self-fulfilling prophecy, especially when this becomes part of social conditioning.

There are many examples in life that dispute the idea that we are somehow destined to live a dysfunctional life if we had a dysfunctional childhood; for example, why do some people who were abused as children grow up to become abusers, while some go on to help others? In his book *A Child Called It*, Dave Pelzer describes the extreme abuse he suffered from his mother. Some of what he writes is hard to comprehend. In fact, when I read the book, I cried all night! Yet despite all the trauma that Pelzer suffered, somehow he found the inner resources to grow into an adult who passionately helps others. And examples like this exist everywhere – people who take their pain and suffering and use it for good.

In *Welcoming the Unwelcome*, Pema Chödrön opens with a chapter entitled 'Start with a broken heart'. Here, she explains that to follow the path of a *Bodhisattva*, we must first embrace our own suffering and pain. In Buddhism a *Bodhisattva* is an ordinary person who is committed to living their lives beyond their own narrow desires. They focus on the good of all beings. To be fully available to others, we must first accept that we are innately good, despite our past and even our transgressions. When we look at some of the most inspiring people in history, we might notice that the one thing many have in common is a past full of suffering and difficulty. One such example is Nelson Mandela who despite enduring a lifetime of discrimination and twenty-five years in prison went on to change the history of his country. Frida Kahlo is an iconic Mexican artist whose life was plagued with trauma, including being seriously injured after a bus accident. Her paintings often depict the female experience and are highly regarded for giving women a voice in a world that was predominantly male.

While we don't want to suffer, and certainly no child should, the wider question here is, if we are predetermined by our genes or by the story of our childhood, then what causes one person to go in one direction and another in the opposite, even though their experiences are similar? Why do siblings growing up in the same household, with the same parents, end up leading completely different lives, with very different values?

Is it possible that there is more in the innate characteristics that we inherit than we give credit to? The works of people like Mark Wolynn in *It Didn't Start With You: How Inherited Family Trauma Shapes Who We Are and How to End the Cycle* and Bessel van der Kolk in *The Body Keeps the Score* make the case that we are not born empty vessels, which contradicts much of the established psychology and science. And although Wolynn and van der Kolk focus on the idea that we inherit past trauma, on the flip side, it also implies that we must also inherit our predecessors' positive qualities. The point here is to keep in mind that our attachments are not just formed by our childhood; sometimes they go back further than that.

But what is attachment?

In 2020, one of my personal Buddhist teachers, Venerable Robina Courtin, gave a talk about love versus attachment. In this talk Ven. Courtin made the point that we tend to think of attachment as a good thing – something we learn through conventional psychology, such as those discussed previously. She goes on to explain that in Buddhist psychology, attachment is the opposite of love; attachment is negative, while love is positive. Of course, I'm not implying that conventional psychology says that love and attachment are the same. However, it fails to clearly differentiate between the two. This then translates into our collective narrative as love and attachment go hand in hand. In fact, Levine and Heller dedicate a chapter in their book, *Attached*, to the topic 'Dependency is not a bad word'. There isn't enough room here to explore this view in detail, but it is worth looking at this short paragraph from their book, under the title 'The co-dependency myth':

"Today's experts offer advice that goes something like this: Your happiness is something that should come from within and should not be dependent on your lover or mate. Your well-being is not their responsibility, and theirs is not yours."

They go on to say, "The basic premise underlying this point of view is that the ideal relationship is one between two self-sufficient people who unite in a mature, respectful way while maintaining clear boundaries."

They also argue that being confident as an individual depends on finding the "right person to depend on" and that "our partners powerfully affect our ability to thrive in the world".

I find Levine and Heller's points disturbing. One, because they degrade the role of the father in a child's development – something that tends to support a patriarchal society and is outdated by any standards. And there are many studies to show just how important a father is in the healthy upbringing of a child; I can vouch for that. Also, their presumption that for relationships to be healthy, partners should depend on each other undermines the importance of independence and self-sufficiency. Once again this is proof of how science and psychology seem to point towards personal agendas.

## The glorification of relationships

Our upbringing in society often emphasises the importance of romantic relationships while undervaluing the significance of individual self-reliance, personal development and autonomy. Conversely, we are often taught that being single past a certain age equates to failure.

Everywhere we turn, the message is the same: being part of a couple is the ideal, whereas being single is sad. The prevailing narrative in modern society is that of one man, one woman and two point something children.

It has somewhat changed with the acceptance of same-sex marriages and relationships. However, with 42% of the population now single and many others in dysfunctional relationships, is it possible that this view of love and relationships is no longer relevant?

So how does the pressure of coupledom affect us in reality?

On the subject of marriage, in her book, *Women Don't Owe You Pretty*, Florence Given asks, "Is it something you've always wanted to do, or is it something you've always been told you wanted to do?"

It is worth considering this question with the courage to accept that we are often blinded by stories of romantic weddings and the happy ever after, therefore it is difficult to know when we are making decisions based on what we want or what others want for us.

Why is it we rarely hear about happy, successful single people? And why is the idea of choosing to stay single or even not to have children considered either selfish or strange?

Well of course it's because that goes against the norm, and anything that might challenge social norms is a threat. Change is always a threat. And as I have already discussed, there are many reasons for keeping with the status quo – the most important one being to make sure we behave.

I recently watched *Maid* on Netflix, a true account of a single mother who ran away from an abusive partner with her little daughter but in so doing was thrown into poverty and became homeless. What struck me most was how the people in her life sat back and watched her being abused, including her own father, even blaming his daughter for her husband's behaviour. Although I never experienced physical abuse, I was made to feel that my husband behaved the way he did because I wasn't a good wife. And I often believed it, because that's what I learned as I was growing up: girls should make sure boys are happy.

These messages are everywhere – in the books we read to our children, the songs we listen to and the films we watch. Girls are taught to focus on their appearance because that's how you get your man. These stories are so embedded in our psyche that we don't recognise dysfunctional relationships.

Even though we have made progress in regard to women's rights, there is an ever-increasing focus on the sexualisation of young girls that is perhaps even more damaging because the messages are so subtle. The results aren't always obvious.

In *Frozen*, Olaf announces, "Love is putting someone else's needs before yours." But is it? And while we may think that the Cinderella complex is specifically harmful to girls, it also impacts how boys grow up thinking about who they should be.

In their book, *The White Knight Syndrome: Rescuing Yourself from Your Need to Rescue Others*, Mary C. Lamia and Marilyn J. Krieger give another useful psychological perspective that influences our beliefs around love. They define white knight syndrome as "a compulsive need to be the rescuer in an intimate relationship originating from early life experiences that left you feeling damaged, guilty, shamed or afraid".

The term 'white knight' sounds like it should apply to men but, in reality, we can all be victims to feeling we must rescue a loved one. In the end, it all comes down to how you perceive yourself and the roles you have become attached to. If you go back through the stories you've heard and the narratives that have been shared throughout your life, you might better understand why you feel you have to rescue others, while letting yourself sink.

I am heartened to see that society is beginning to challenge some of the narratives that we have grown up believing. I am hopeful that our next stage of evolution will give space for us to authentically explore who we truly are in terms of love.

## Is it natural for humans to be in monogamous relationships?

The question of whether it is natural for humans to be monogamous is a subject of ongoing debate among scientists, anthropologists and psychologists.

From an evolutionary standpoint, monogamy has been observed in some species of primates, including humans. Monogamy may have emerged in early humans as a way to ensure the survival of offspring and to create social bonds that were beneficial for group living.

However, it is also worth noting that humans are a highly adaptable species and while monogamy is a common cultural norm in many societies, there are also societies where polygamy or other forms of non-monogamous relationships are accepted or even encouraged.

Ultimately, whether monogamy is "natural" for humans is a complex question that likely has no single answer. Some individuals may be more predisposed towards monogamous relationships, while others may prefer non-monogamous relationships. Additionally, societal and cultural norms can also influence the prevalence and acceptance of monogamy within a given community or population.

Monogamy evolved as a way for society to become more efficient. In paired relationships, it can be easier to care for children, share resources and build social networks. People who are able to maintain a long-term relationship do so because they adapt as time passes. They accept that romantic love might have faded and the desire for sex may have diminished, because their love for each other matures. However, for many, that's not always possible, especially when sexual desire plays a prominent role in their life. And then there is the question of a longing to fulfil a personal dream that requires you to be either single or no longer in that relationship.

The truth is, to procreate we must pair up, but that is very different to the social narrative telling us that to be happy, we must be in a monogamous relationship that lasts until we die.

Research might suggest that people who are in a committed relationship and live with a partner tend to live longer than those who are single. Studies have shown that people who are married or in long-term relationships tend to have lower rates of mortality and better overall health compared to those who are single. One possible reason for this is that living with a partner may provide social support, reduce stress and encourage healthy behaviours.

However, it is important to note that these studies do not necessarily prove causation and there are many other factors that may influence a person's health and lifespan.

Later in this book, we will look at this in more detail to explore the real reasons people in, say, 'blue zones' live longer, and you might be surprised to find out that it's not necessarily because they are in a relationship. Blue zones are geographic areas where people live exceptionally long and healthy lives, like Sardinia in Italy and Okinawa in Japan. They have been characterised by traditional lifestyles, nutritious diets and strong social connections.

## Why ending a relationship isn't failure

In the first few days following my break-up, the idea I'd have to explain to people that my marriage was over and it was because he cheated was embarrassing. I tried to avoid going out or at least going to places we'd usually go together. Then I had a conversation that changed all that. An old family friend who I knew was in a very unhealthy marriage decided to offer her twopence. A couple of years earlier, she'd found out her husband was having an affair and she was very vocal in letting the world know how disgusted she was with him. I'm not sure there was anyone she didn't tell. But despite all her unhappiness, she decided to stay in her marriage.

I'm not judging her. It was her choice and I respect that, but when she found out I had decided to end my marriage, she told me I had chosen the easy way out. At that time, I was selling the family home, already without a job after my redundancy and packing thirty years of life into a few boxes, so the idea that my decision was the easy one made me angry. Surely it would have been easier to just ignore the cheating and keep my life as it was. However, once I'd settled into my new life, I reflected on this conversation and realised that perhaps she was right, because having to live a lie is far more difficult than starting a life where you are free to be yourself.

So why do we view the ending of a relationship as failure instead of giving it the respect it needs?

I recently watched a documentary where Jennifer Lopez talked about her divorce from husband Marc Anthony. Their marriage was idealised – two successful Latin American superstars, clearly in love and with two children. Their split came as a shock to many who followed their lives because it seemed perfect and yet it ended. However, Lopez said they have continued to be friends and there is still love between them.

The idea that for a relationship to be meaningful or real it must last forever is part of the happily-ever-after story. However, as I can confirm, all relationships are meaningful – even, or especially in some cases, the ones that end.

Real love is knowing when to let someone go and not staying because of fear or comfort. Real self-love is knowing how to honour yourself and accepting when it's time to move on. Heartbreak might feel like a death but if you know what to do with it, eventually it can lead to immense personal growth. Well, that has been my experience anyway.

The biggest failure in life is to live it as if you have forever. If you've been brave enough to walk away from a relationship that no was no longer working, then you should give yourself the respect you deserve. Furthermore, if you have made the decision to prioritise your personal aspirations or pursue a path that deviates from the traditional happy-ending fairy tale, you deserve significant recognition because what you have done requires courage! And even if it wasn't your decision to end your relationship and you are still struggling with it, know that the sun will shine again. It may even shine brighter.

## Can you really be single and still be happy?

After my divorce, I rented a beautiful two-bed in an area of London I had always wanted to return to. It was where I lived before my parents' divorce. For the first couple of days, I had to sleep on a blow-up mattress because my new bed hadn't arrived yet. It felt strange to be in this place, alone, and yet I remember also feeling a sense of excitement about my new life. In that space of unfamiliarity was also opportunity, because with the old path now gone, I had the chance to carve out a new future on my own terms. And I guess this is an important point: everything in life is determined by our perspective, just as I covered earlier in the book. Of course you should cry if that's how you are feeling and of course you should acknowledge the disappointment and sadness, but somewhere along the line, you must turn it into an opportunity to start over.

What I've gained from being thrust back into the world as a single person far outweighs the life I was living. I'm not saying this is how everyone should live, nor am I saying being in a relationship is bad, but there may be times in your life when you need to be alone. Sometimes, being in a relationship can hold you back because however loving it may be, there will always be some kind of compromise and it is time to give being single equal respect. But more importantly, it is also time we accepted that, like most things in life, there are no guarantees that any relationship will last forever or that it should. The most important relationship is the one we have with ourselves; this is the one that we must nurture and develop. Learning how to be by yourself is perhaps the greatest lesson of all because, like it or not, there may very well be a time when you will be alone.

I thought it would be good to end this section with some examples of people who never married and yet lived happy, successful lives. Just to note: I'm not saying you shouldn't get married or be in a relationship. I do, however, want to give equal respect to living your life as you wish and not being indoctrinated to pursue a life because that is what is expected.

**Louisa May Alcott** grew up with more freedom and education than the average girl in the mid-19th century. Though she wrote more than two hundred works, she is best known for her novel *Little Women*. Alcott had no desire to get married and wanted the same for the fictional version of herself, Jo March. Unfortunately, her publisher insisted she marry the character off at the end of her iconic book, and that's the ending we know today.

**Bryan Stevenson** is a renowned American lawyer and social justice activist made famous for securing the release of many wrongly imprisoned individuals. He is quoted as saying that his career is "incompatible with married life".

After years of being ignored by history in favour of shining the spotlight on Thomas Edison, inventor **Nikola Tesla** is finally getting some attention and recognition nearly eighty years after his death. Though best known for designing the alternating current (AC) electrical system and the Tesla coil, he was also known for some of his quirks. For instance, not only did he decide not to marry, he also opted to remain celibate, claiming it helped him be more creative. Tesla did, however, profess to have had a relationship with a pigeon, once saying, "I loved that pigeon as a man loves a woman, and she loved me. As long as I had her, there was a purpose to my life."

As one of the most famous nurses in the world, **Florence Nightingale** cared for a lot of people, but that didn't include a husband. Though she had numerous suitors throughout her life and at least two marriage proposals, she decided not to marry, believing that God had chosen her to work and serve others as a single woman. She summed up her reasoning for rejecting a marriage proposal in a diary entry she wrote when she was seventeen: "I have a moral, an active nature which requires satisfaction and that I would not find in his life. I could be satisfied to spend a life with him in combining our different powers to some great object. I could not satisfy this nature by spending a life with him in making society and arranging domestic things."

Most people associate **Jane Austen's** books with love and romance, but unlike many of the characters in her novels, she never married. It's not as though she didn't have the opportunity to wed: Austen actually had several suitors and a few marriage proposals – one of which even ended in an engagement that she broke off after one day. Though her exact reasons to remain single are unknown, some speculate that she didn't want to relinquish any of her writing time, money or success to married life, and made choices that would allow her to retain her career and autonomy.

And one of my favourites, because she has inspired me, is **Diane Keaton**.

While she starred in several classic romantic comedies, including *Annie Hall* and *Something's Gotta Give*, Diane Keaton never married in real life. That said, she has had high-profile romances with stars like Al Pacino and Warren Beatty, and she adopted two children. But she doesn't have any regrets, she told the Associated Foreign Press in a 2019 interview: "I don't think about it a lot, but I'm aware of the fact that I'm unusual in that regard, and maybe I did miss out on something—but then, nobody can have everything, right? I'm not unhappy."

I hope that the preceding pages have conveyed the message that regardless of whether you opt for marriage, a romantic relationship or to be single it's crucial to ensure that your decision aligns with your genuine desires, rather than conforming to societal expectations.

But how do you know you're doing what you want and not what you've been conditioned to think you want?

The following introspective activity could prove beneficial to help you understand what propels you towards a specific course of action.

> **Reflection on relationships: part two**
>
> Thinking back to the self-reflection exercise on page 90, look at the answers you wrote to the following questions:
>
> - What story dominates my family character?
> - How does that continue in my own life?
>
> Now thinking about what we have covered on fairy tales, has anything changed for you?
>
> Can you honestly say the choices you made were yours? If not, what will you do going forward?
>
> Spend a little time reflecting on yourself in your relationships and write down whatever comes up.
>
> If you need to take a little time out before continuing, please do, otherwise let's continue by looking at the topic of sex.

## Why Is Sex a Problem?

Before we delve into the subject, it is helpful to first distinguish between sex and intimacy.

Sex is a physical act involving the erogenous zones of the human body typically associated with reproduction and pleasure. It can take many forms and can involve a wide range of sexual activities.

Sexual activity is a normal and healthy part of human sexuality, and it can have a variety of physical and emotional benefits such as stress relief, pleasure and intimacy. Sexuality and sexual practices can vary widely depending on cultural, social and personal factors.

Intimacy refers to a close and personal connection between two individuals that involves emotional, physical and/or intellectual sharing. It can take many forms, including deep conversations, shared experiences, physical touch and sexual activity. Intimacy involves vulnerability and trust, and it often requires a level of openness and honesty that may not be present in other types of relationship.

Intimacy can be an important aspect of human connection and can contribute to feelings of happiness, fulfilment and well-being. It can also be challenging to cultivate, particularly in the face of societal pressures or personal barriers such as past traumas or insecurities.

It's important to note that intimacy is not limited to romantic or sexual relationships, and can be present in friendships, familial relationships and other types of interpersonal connections. Building and maintaining intimacy often requires effort, communication and a willingness to be vulnerable and empathetic towards others.

## Desire and lust

In today's society, which often places a heavy emphasis on sexuality, it can be difficult to discern whether we are motivated by authentic attraction or an urge to fulfil uncontrollable lust.

Lust is a strong feeling of sexual desire or an intense longing for someone or something. It is often associated with a physical attraction or craving for sexual pleasure. Lust can be a normal and healthy part of human sexuality, but it can also be problematic if it leads to harmful behaviour or interferes with an individual's ability to form and maintain healthy relationships.

Lust can be experienced in a variety of ways, ranging from a passing attraction or fantasy to a more intense and persistent desire. It can be directed towards a particular person or object and may be influenced by physical or psychological factors such as hormones, past experiences or cultural norms.

If we associate sex solely with feelings of lust and an insatiable craving, akin to an addiction, we risk overlooking the true benefits sex can offer.

## When sex gets confused with love

Earlier, we examined the question: what is love? and explored various perspectives on the topic. We noted that Hinduism and ancient Greek philosophy view sex as a positive aspect of human life, whereas the Judeo-Christian tradition regards it as a sinful act.

According to the teachings of Tantric Buddhism, experiencing a genuine orgasm results in a temporary state of non-existence, not only for oneself but also for the other person. The Tibetan *Book of the Dead* describes how a complete orgasm can offer a glimpse of clear light, a sensation typically reserved for specific circumstances such as near-death experiences.

If sex is such a joyful experience, why is it often so problematic?

Revisiting the account of the married man I met who shared his perspective on extramarital sex sheds light on why considering sex as an escape can lead to complications. Given that the media often portrays sex in this manner, it is not surprising that many of us are uncertain about its role in our lives.

Intimate relationships require us to blend elements of friendship, partnership, companionship and erotic love, creating a significant burden to sustain something that can be unrealistic. In our twenties our love is often founded on physical attraction. However, as time progresses, not only do our bodies change, but our shared experiences can also alter how we perceive our partner. If we no longer feel that closeness or, worse, lose the physical attraction, we may either suppress those feelings or search for alternative ways to express them.

For many individuals, a loss of sexual attraction or desire towards their partner is the cause of relationship breakdown.

In her book *Mating in Captivity: How to Keep Desire and Passion Alive in Long-term Relationships* renowned couples therapist Esther Perel explores the tension between the need for familiarity and mystery in romantic relationships. Her advice centres around the understanding that "love rests on surrender and autonomy" – in other words, the need for togetherness with the space for separateness.

Perel astutely acknowledges the modern-day challenge placed upon relationships, which is the expectation for them to provide the same level of fulfilment that was once derived from a tightly knit community. She points out that, in the past, our sense of grounding, meaning and continuity came from the collective support of an entire village. However, in today's world, we place an additional burden on our committed relationships, seeking not only romance but also emotional and sexual fulfilment. With this in mind, Perel poses the thought-provoking question: "Is it any surprise that so many relationships crumble under the weight of these immense expectations?"

And, most interestingly, Perel adds: "The grand illusion of committed love is that we think our partners are ours."

The notion that we have ownership over another person due to being in a committed relationship can be traced back to when men considered their wives as their property. Although it may not be immediately apparent today, this model of ownership remains ingrained in the institution of marriage.

I remember proudly wearing my wedding ring and never taking it off. To me, it symbolised that I was spoken for and because of that I felt worthy. After all, I grew up in a culture that taught me a woman's ultimate goal should be to get married and anything else was failure. Being married felt secure and it meant I no longer had to play the exhausting game of trying to attract a man.

However, I failed to recognise, as Perel so aptly points out, that "exchanging passion for stability is essentially trading one fiction for another. Both are products of our imagination." In essence, once we settle for comfort and stability in our relationships, it becomes challenging to sustain the passion.

Following my divorce, I found myself back in the dating "game" and it soon dawned on me how much sex had grown dull and uninspiring in my marriage. I'm not suggesting this is always the case, but I would wager a bet that it is for many. And given the importance of sex in our lives, it is no surprise that so many marriages end in divorce, citing infidelity as the reason.

While writing this section of the book, I came to the realisation that the topic of sex is vast. Therefore, I acknowledge that these few paragraphs are insufficient to do justice to this complex subject. However, I hope to have given you enough food for thought to help you challenge your views on sex and how they might be affecting you in your relationships.

Before we move on to the next part of the book, let's reflect on your experiences and views on sex.

> **Reflection on sex**
>
> It's important to find a quiet place to do this reflection and to have the courage to be open with yourself when you answer the following questions. You don't have to share this with anyone, so be as honest as you can with yourself.
>
> - What are your views on sex?
>
>   Do you think it's important? Not important? Or maybe you don't have a view at all.
>
> - What were the conversations about sex like in your family and in your community when you were growing up, and how did this transpire in your life?
>
> - Have you fully explored your sexuality, or do you feel inhibited?
>
> - Is this an area in your life that you would like to change, and, if so, how?
>
> These questions are only meant to help you start to explore your relationship with sex and how it has affected you in your relationships. The more

open and honest you are, the more you'll be able to gain insights about the role of sex in your life so you can identify what might need to change. More importantly, as this journey we are on together is to help you reconnect with your true self, knowing what you want and who you are from a sexuality perspective is fundamental.

I suggest you come back to this again later or, if it turns out this is something you feel you need support for, you might want to work with me directly or see a therapist.

## Section summary

### Key points:

- Relationships are not one-dimensional and because of that they are often complicated.
- The reason why love can be difficult to understand is because we confuse it with desire and attachment.
- Our views of love, relationships and sex are formed from a young age and are dependent on our cultural and social background.
- Sex, lust, desire and intimacy are frequently interconnected, despite their distinct definitions in our lives.

Now it's time to move on to a whole new topic and to delve into how our education, work and money experiences shape our life.

## Being Schooled

In Part One I discussed how a part of the societal story we learn as we grow up involves leading a linear life that resembles the diagram below.

Good education → Secure job → Life partner → Nice home & car → Family → Bigger house - holidays! → Retire - happy ever after!

However, the truth is that life is never that tidy. In fact, it's usually quite a mess. Remember this?

## Real Life

While this story of a linear life is instilled in us before we start school, it is consistently reinforced through the formal education system.

I worked in the education sector for over a decade – as a classroom teacher, a curriculum leader and national education adviser – so I've experienced the whole spectrum. I brought up three boys who went through the state education system, much the same as myself back in the 1970s and '80s. To say I have an opinion on the education system is an understatement. It is something I feel extremely passionate about because it has such an impact on our lives. However, I won't spend too long here going into the fundamental flaws in our school system because it really would take up most of the book. In short, in my view, the education system is outdated and no longer fit for purpose, especially since the real world has changed dramatically.

I grew up in a culturally diverse community in North London, which gave me an early appreciation that, regardless of our ethnic or religious background, we are all fundamentally the same. We share the same fears, needs and aspirations. It is these common traits that truly define us as humans.

When I started school, my English was limited because my parents had only come to the UK a couple of years before I was born, so we spoke Greek at home. In those days, children who were bilingual were often isolated from the rest of the pupils – something that made me feel different and excluded. I finished school with no formal qualifications and yet, despite all that, I still managed to do well in life. I seemed to have a knack for convincing people I was up to the task, even landing my first real job for the Ministry of Defence.

In my late thirties I went to university and managed to achieve a first-class honours degree in computer science, while raising three children. I continued my studies, eventually completing two post-graduate degrees. I kept my old school reports to remind me of what I have achieved in spite of comments like "Anna is not intellectually mature enough for higher education. She should consider getting a secretarial job!" By the way, the teacher who wrote that comment usually slept through my lessons because he didn't think his class was worth the effort and yet he felt qualified to comment on my chances of doing well in the future.

When you think back to your schooling, did you have similar experiences? Well, we'll explore this in more detail in the reflection exercise later. For now, I'd like to share a few examples I've personally witnessed as a teacher to highlight the failings of the British education system.

Throughout my teaching career I'd see one bright, creative child after another labelled as "underperforming" or "special needs" because they didn't quite fit the requirements. School, it seems, is still very much a factory with the sole function of creating productive adults who will go out into the world to maintain the status quo, except for a few mavericks who dare to break the rules.

I'm reminded of a girl I taught who came from a terribly abusive background; both her parents were addicts. She was an extremely bright girl and although she missed a lot of her schooling, she managed to get great exam results. But a year after leaving school, she came to see me, already a single mother. On the opposite end of the scale was a girl who loved to dance, a star in all the school performances and responsible for some impressive choreography. Her dream was to be a dancer, but her parents insisted she go to university to study law. In the end, she gave up fighting her parents and followed their dream. A few years later, I bumped into her on the Tube and asked her what she was doing with her life. "I studied law but couldn't get a job so I'm temping at the moment," she replied with a rather sad look on her face, that sparkle I once knew already lost. And my heart broke for her lost dreams.

Another ex-student was a keen boxer. When he talked about boxing, he came alive, but his parents wanted him to go to university. As a mother, I completely understand his parents' concerns; however, what they failed to recognise was that their son was not academic. He struggled to complete work to a high enough standard when at school because his mind was elsewhere – his dreams were in the boxing ring. I don't know what happened after school, but I have a sneaky suspicion his parents might have won.

In my first year of teaching, I was given a group of students who were not entered for exams. There were no expectations on me to get them a qualification and, in the beginning, I was happy to go with that. However, I soon realised that unless I challenged them, I'd have to put up with their poor behaviour for a year! So, one day I asked them a serious question: "Do you want to get a GCSE in this subject?"

They looked confused and for a few minutes stayed silent. Then one of the boys replied, "We can't because we're not clever enough." His response upset me because this is what had been drummed into them throughout their school life. Then I offered them a choice: "If you promise to work hard, really hard, I promise to work hard with you, and you will pass. But you must do exactly what I tell you; you have to get the work done on time and no more messing around in the class."

They didn't respond immediately. Then, one by one, they all, bar one, agreed. They worked hard as promised and I kept at them every lesson. Thankfully it paid off, because as a new teacher, the last thing I needed was to have bad results! All of them passed and it was one of the proudest moments in my teaching career. However, just as I thought it was over, they told me they were staying on for the sixth form and had signed up for my class. Guess I couldn't get rid of them! A year later, I moved to another school on promotion.

On my last day, as I was walking to my car, I could see a large pink piece of card stuck on my windscreen. *Blasted kids*, I thought. *They've trashed my car!!* When I reached the bonnet, I took the card and was ready to throw it away, when I suddenly realised there was a message on it.

"You are the best, thank you for everything."

Each of my "reject" class had written me a personal message. This made me a little emotional and it reminded me of what one of the boys had said to me earlier that day: "Ms, we are screwed because nobody will care about us when you are gone!"

I share this with you to highlight the point that this story is not unusual. It happens often in schools. Perhaps you've even experienced it yourself. This illustrates that in life sometimes we get lucky and meet someone who believes in us, which gives us a different perspective, maybe even directing us on a path we never knew we could take. Life isn't always just about hard work; sometimes it's about being in the right place at the right time. If you understand this, you can learn how to put yourself in the right place or, at the very least, you can learn how to recognise an opportunity when it presents itself.

When I was teaching, I came up with a theory that there are four types of children (there are way more in reality but humour me, please!). I classify them as follows:

1. **The highly engaged child** – very well prepared for the education system and eager to learn. These children work hard and usually do well in school. Teachers quite like them. They make our job easier.

2. **The invisible child** – comes to school and keeps their head down because they don't want to be noticed and so they usually aren't. These children achieve average at best. Teachers don't mind them; they are easy to ignore.

3. **The refuser** – doesn't want to be in school, usually has a troubled home life, poor focus and an inability to complete classwork. Teachers dread these students because they demand 90% of their attention.

4. **The insightful child** – bright, maybe creative but not in the conventionally recognised way. They may not do well at school because they don't fit in but they fly when they are set free. These children don't even exist as far as the education system is concerned. (P.S. That was me!)

In 2007, Sir Ken Robinson gave an inspiring and insightful TED Talk about education in which he said, "We squander children's creativity, and get educated out of creativity."

He makes the point that our education system was built to meet the needs of an industrialised society. And because of the overall purpose of education, we discourage children from following subjects they might enjoy because they are seen as less desirable – in other words, less likely to get them a job. So priority is given to subjects such as maths, science and languages, with the arts usually bottom of the hierarchy of subjects because artists don't make money, or at least that is the common view.

As a result of this viewpoint, we're led to believe that academic achievement and even IQ tests are valid indicators of intelligence. However, they're not entirely dependable markers of intelligence; they simply show how well someone has learned to repeat, memorise and recall information.

Creativity and entrepreneurship, two characteristics that drive innovation, are often undervalued and not given adequate recognition. Strangely enough, these traits are frequently overlooked despite their significant impact.

Intelligence is diverse and difficult to define accurately. Even the most renowned scientists, psychologists and other experts cannot agree on one definition. So, we can accurately deduce that intelligence is a matter of perspective. In fact, I'd go as far as to say that intelligence depends on our experience. Unless we have some physical defect that prevents us from learning, we all have the capacity to grow. Intelligence, like most things, is not static. It can change depending on how much of it we use. Therefore, labelling a child as intelligent or not from a very young age can create a self-fulfilling prophecy. And, ultimately, we become what we believe, which is very much the theme covered in this book.

Sir Robinson made a valuable point when he said, "If you are not prepared to be wrong, then you will never come up with anything original. By the time kids become adults, they lose their ability to be wrong because making mistakes is stigmatised."

Some of the most incredibly brilliant and creative individuals struggled in school and it wasn't until they left the education system and had time to recover from their schooling that they discovered their true potential.

Many of us spend the rest of our lives trying to get over our education. Wouldn't it be better to teach children how to manage risk rather than how to play it safe? How different would our world be if we respected dance, art, music and other creative subjects as much as maths and science? I know it sounds romantic rather than practical; however, I think there is a bigger agenda that drives our education system, and it certainly doesn't have our children at the heart of it.

While the subject of intelligence and education is undoubtedly complex, I hope this brief discussion has given you something to think about, particularly regarding your personal educational experience and how it may have shaped your self-beliefs. As you engage in the next reflection exercise, you may find it useful to reflect on these ideas.

## The story of Gillian Lynne

I'd like to end this section with a true story about a lady called Gillian Lynne. When Gillian was a young girl she struggled in school, barely able to sit still and focus on her lessons. Her teachers identified her as problematic and told her mother to take her to a doctor. At the appointment, the mother explained her daughter's problem to the doctor who, after a while, looked at Gillian and said, "I need to discuss all of this with your mother in private, so you stay in here while I go outside with your mother."

On his way out, the doctor turned his radio on and left Gillian with the music playing. When the adults walked out of the room, the doctor turned towards the mother and said, "Just watch your daughter." They both turned to see Gillian dancing. The doctor then said, "There is nothing wrong with your daughter. She is a dancer. Take her to dance school."

And that is exactly what her mother did. Gillian Lynne became a successful dancer, actress and choreographer. She worked on Broadway as a choreographer for *Cats* and *The Phantom of the Opera*. What would have happened to Gillian had she not visited that doctor? Would she have been put on medication, labelled dysfunctional all her life, killing all her creativity and depriving the world of a true talent?

History is full of stories like that of Gillian Lynne. Even Einstein was thought to have learning disabilities as a young child. He was slow to learn and talk and avoided other children. He also had terrible tantrums. He dropped out of school at fifteen because he hated rote learning and the discipline style of his teachers. But as we all know, he had a great imagination and a thirst for exploring. Being in a classroom, sat in front of a teacher reading out of a Bible all day would have been torture for someone like Einstein.

It's interesting to note that in a recent interview, Michelle Obama recounted an experience where her careers adviser told her that she was not suitable for Princeton. However, she proved them wrong by attending the university. This serves as a reminder to be sceptical of the advice we receive, even if it comes from someone who is considered an expert. When asked how she overcame being stereotyped, Obama advised young women in the audience to develop a strong self-belief that does not require external confirmation of their abilities.

Now that you have gained some insight into the depth of your education, do you feel it may be beneficial to become somewhat 'unschooled'? I hope you do, and that's something I'll guide you through in the following pages.

> **Reflection on your education**
>
> Find a quiet place, with soft lighting, and sit comfortably. Close your eyes and take a few slow breaths in and out. Let your thoughts pass through without giving them too much attention and allow your body to relax, without falling asleep or becoming drowsy. The point is to stay alert and clear.
>
> Take yourself back to your days at school. Imagine yourself as a young child in your classroom and see if you can feel what it was like back then.
>
> Then drop the following questions into your mind:
>
> - What sort of student were you?
> - Did you enjoy school?
> - If not, why?
> - If yes, why?
>
> When you are ready, take your notebook but stay in the same state of mind.

Write a short description of yourself as a school pupil. Give yourself the labels you think represent you while you were young.

For example: I am clever, hardworking, sporty, not sporty, artistic, not artistic, can't run, unlikeable, pleaser and any other labels you can think of.

Once you have written them down, reflect on what you have written. Is anything surprising to you? How does it play out in your life today?

You'll find additional support for these reflections on my website, annazannides.com

## Section summary

### Key points:

- The education system is designed to teach us how to fit into the working world.
- Our school experiences influence our self-belief and what we think we can achieve in our lifetimes.
- Intelligence is a subjective concept that cannot be accurately measured.
- Creativity and entrepreneurship are undervalued and this can stifle the progress of many children.

In the next part of the book, we'll look at how this is carried into our working lives as adults.

## Work and Money

We all have an inbuilt warning system whose job it is to remind us of who we truly are. When you become disconnected from it, the signal will keep on sounding until you turn to face your truth.

I tried to ignore the signs but near the time of my redundancy and divorce those messages no longer just sat gently below the surface; they started to shout louder at the most unexpected times, forcing me to face truths I'd denied for a long time.

These two stories were my reminders:

### Party in the park

It was a rather pleasant, warmish day in London. I was at my work's head office, which was in a prestigious building just off Tottenham Court Road, a few minutes' walk from Goodge Street station – as Central London as you can get. It was always full of people going about their business, rushing to get to work, rushing to get lunch, then rushing to get back home, only to repeat it all again the next day.

Opposite the office block was a small park that we would sneak out to for a quick smoke and, ironically, to get some fresh air! On this day, the park was busier than usual because one thing us Londoners like to do is take advantage of a non-raining day – because who knows when the next one will come along. I was going through a difficult patch in my life. Redundancy was hanging over my head and things at home were worsening. This little park became my escape, a place for me to stand and stare, just for a moment.

I had a usual spot where I could stand and be sure I couldn't be seen from the office windows – just in case any of the bigwigs caught me taking a break without asking their permission. I lit my cigarette and felt a little bit of the stress subside. As I stood there, lost in thought, I noticed one of the benches had been turned into a buffet table, laden with an assortment of crumbled muffins, a few packets of crisps and a fair share of tinned beer. And in the background, music played from a 1990s ghetto blaster.

Then, out of nowhere, someone shouted:

"Don't touch our food! You can't have any."

I turned towards the voice. It was a thin, scruffy man who I could tell was homeless. *Is he talking to me?* I thought. Yes, it appeared he was. I wasn't welcome to the party, and certainly not allowed to share the party delights. I was a little startled by his reaction to me. Then, out of nowhere I was overcome by a deep sadness. At first, I thought it was because I felt sorry for this man and his friends, having to live like this – what caused them to end up on the streets? But then I realised, it wasn't sadness for these street people; it was envy.

I mean, how dare they be partying and enjoying life at 11am on a working day? That feeling I'd been having a lot recently hit me again. I felt trapped. Damn that stupid career, all the things I owned and the marriage I dared not think too much about. At that moment, all I wanted was to join in, to have fun and be irresponsible. There was a sense of loss. Who was this person standing here, in this body? But once again, like a good girl, I put out my cigarette, stuck a piece of gum in my mouth to cover the smell and walked back into my life.

Later that year I had a similar experience, or perhaps I should call it a wake-up call.

## The train

I'd begun to look forward to the long train journeys to meetings across the country as an education adviser, because they felt like 'me time'.

I'd grab a good organic coffee from Pret at Euston Station, and if I was feeling extremely self-indulgent, I'd treat myself to a fresh croissant, ignoring the extra calories. Then, I'd find a seat by the window. Sometimes, if I was lucky, it would be in First Class, and then I'd sit back to watch the world flash by.

One day I was making my way to Birmingham for a 9am meeting, so I had an extremely early start, which had become the norm for me. I settled in for the relatively short journey of a little more than an hour, fixed my earphones into my ears and closed my eyes for a while. I turned up the volume to drown out the conversations going on around me and then 'At This Moment' by Michael Bublé started to play.

Outside the window, one green patch after another flashed past. Occasionally, a few sheep would appear and, above, the sky was overshadowed by those all too familiar grey clouds. Then I noticed a sadness, similar to the one I'd experienced a few days earlier in the park.

I should have been happy. I had it all but, although I couldn't quite work out what was wrong with my life, I knew something was fundamentally wrong. Why had Bublé's words touched me so much on that day? Why was I jealous of the homeless man in the park? I was trapped living a life that wasn't what I wanted, and turning fifty had given me the wake-up call that there was no more time to play the game anymore.

The voice I kept ignoring was getting louder, the promise I'd made as a young girl kept resurfacing from inside, asking me: "Anna, when will you be who you really are?"

I had come to a point in my life when everything seemed dull and routine. I longed to hear words spoken to me with the same passion and sincerity that Michael Bublé sang about – genuine words of love, not just going through the motions. I realised that I had paid a price for falling into the societal narrative of settling down, getting a good job and starting a family. While this may work for some, and I acknowledge and respect those who have made it work, it doesn't work for everyone. In fact, I dare say it doesn't work for many of us.

The beauty of ageing lies in the understanding that life is finite. This knowledge makes it more important to start living life on your own terms, with a renewed sense of urgency. If this is so crucial, why do we find ourselves so trapped in the narrative of work and money?

I remember when I was studying for my computer science degree, feeling hopeful that one day, with computers, life would become so much easier. However, it's turned out to be quite the opposite. Whereas before, a weekend was an opportunity to totally switch off, nowadays work never stops. We are available 24/7 every day of the year, even when abroad. Is it any surprise there is an epidemic of burn-out and chronic stress?

It hasn't always been this way; we aren't designed to be "workers". You might be thinking, well, we have to work, but while most of us do need to earn an income, it's the value we've placed on our working life that has changed so much. There was a time when we worked to live; now we live to work and that's no accident. As you'll read in the next section, this new way of living was designed on purpose to keep us working harder and longer.

## Conditioned to work

In the early 1900s, society went through a systemic change due to the rise in industrialisation. We had become a society that could produce goods faster than we could consume them. This challenged the very basis of our country's economy – industrialisation meant that supply outperformed demand. Until then, luxury goods had been out of reach for most – the cars, expensive clothes, furniture and other non-essential goods were purely for the rich. Now, faced with factory production, business leaders grew concerned that the economy would collapse. They needed a market for their products.

In 1928, Edward Bernays, one of the pioneers of the public relations industry, wrote in his book *Propaganda* that "Mass production is profitable only if its rhythm can be maintained." He went on to argue that business "cannot afford to wait until the public asks for its product; it must maintain a constant touch, through advertising and propaganda, to assure itself the continuous demand which alone will make its costly plant profitable".

Economist Edward Cowdrick supported the notion that workers should be encouraged to become consumers, introducing the term 'the new economic gospel of consumption'. This idea was also promoted by Hazel Kyrk and Theresa McMahon, economists who believed that people should abandon "thrift and husbandry" and prioritise the acquisition of goods over free time.

Kyrk argued that aspirations should be ever-increasing, stating that "a high standard of living must be dynamic, a progressive standard" based on the envy of those in higher social classes, fuelled by consumption, which would lead to continued economic growth.

Let's just look at this statement again: prioritise goods over free time. Does this sound familiar to you? When we think life is too busy or that we can put off what we want today for some ideal in the future, are we not trading time for goods?

In the following brief tale, Paulo Coelho demonstrates how our perceptions of work and money are hindering us from enjoying our lives in the present.

## The fisherman

During a visit to a small village in Brazil, a prosperous entrepreneur observes a small boat heading towards the shore. The fisherman on the boat has caught a few large fish, which impresses the businessman. Curious, the businessman asks the fisherman how long it took to catch that many fish.

The fisherman responds by saying that it didn't take him very long. However, the businessman persists with his questioning and asks the fisherman why he doesn't stay out longer to catch more fish. He then enquires about how the fisherman spends the rest of his day. The fisherman answers that he goes back home after fishing, spends time playing with his children, takes an afternoon nap, and then enjoys the company of his wife and friends. In the evenings, he plays his guitar, drinks with his friends and they sing and dance throughout the night.

The businessman offers to help the fisherman improve his business so that he can spend more time fishing and catch more fish, enabling him to save enough money to purchase a larger boat. The businessman even proposes the idea that once the fisherman's business expands sufficiently, he could leave the village and live in the city.

The fisherman is puzzled by the suggestion and, after asking a few more questions, the businessman explains that once the fisherman has built up his business and accumulated enough wealth, he could retire to the village and spend his evenings drinking, laughing and dancing.

The fisherman then responds, "Isn't that what I am already doing now?"

This fable accurately describes modern life. We keep working so we can buy more, maybe save a little in the hope that one day we will be free to live our lives. We spend our lives searching for the ideal job, perfect partner or the occasional thrill, so we can feel more alive. Like addicts, we keep on chasing, constantly doing, on a merry-go-round that never seems to stop. The more we feed our addictions, the more insatiable they become.

You only need to watch people on their daily commute to work. People dressed in their formal clothing, rushing to get to a job most don't really enjoy, because we believe it is quite acceptable to live for our weekends and holidays. On the London Underground, people rarely talk to each other; they're usually too busy trying to push past the person in front of them. Then it's the mad scramble for the last seat or the tiny empty space to stand in, while we pretend to be somewhere else rather than on the overcrowded train. But nowadays we are lucky enough to be able to hide in our phones and make believe that none of this is happening.

Then, after a day at the office, we go through the same crazy routine to get back home for a few hours of rest, only to repeat it again the next day. And to make this all bearable, we bury ourselves in drink, food, TV, sex or the next brand spanking new car.

I'm not implying that this is how we live all the time, nor do I think it necessarily applies to everyone. Some people do work that adds purpose and meaning to their lives. However, often we find ourselves in work that doesn't give us much more than an income because we don't always choose our profession based on what we like or enjoy.

The collective narrative places higher value on professions that are money orientated rather than value-based. Those in caring professions such as nurses and teachers are at the bottom of the scale compared to bankers and CEOs of large corporate companies because our society supports the idea that it is money that brings more happiness. And just to clarify: I understand that not everyone is privileged enough to have choices. Sometimes in life you have to just do what you can to get by. However, given a choice, I wonder how many of us would be doing what we do.

I was once part of the daily commute madness. Unlike most people, I found the only way I could survive that gruelling hour-or-so journey was to opt out. Instead of joining in with the crazy rush, I'd leave home early enough to go slow and I'd just let people pass by. I spent a lot of my time observing people, trying to work out what their story was. And sometimes I'd smile at someone, just to see if they would smile back. I soon realised that contrary to what people think of Londoners, most people do return your smile and giving up your seat to someone more needy isn't unusual, even on the overcrowded trains. My commute into London made me see that people are not bad; in fact, they are innately good.

But one thing puzzled me. For the life of me, I could never understand the rush. I mean, most of us can work out how long it will take to get to work – after a couple of trips, we know, right? However, it seemed that most people have a short memory because every day the same people would literally run to catch their train, then do exactly the same on the way home. I often asked myself, "Why? Do they oversleep every day? Did their alarm clock not go off again?"

I later concluded that people get caught up in the daily rush for various reasons – some because they just can't get out of bed on time, others because they are awful at planning their day. But I observed a strange sort of behaviour that I attribute to a sense of self-importance gained through the status a job might give us. People who become so attached to these roles that they believe them to be who they are. Using this sense of self-importance, we feel entitled to push past someone, to shove them out of the way and to take the last seat.

Under these conditions we get to see how human behaviour reflects just how caught up we have become in the labels assigned to us by what we do, rather than who we are: *I am a teacher, an accountant, lawyer or whatever else...* We meet someone for the first time and, undoubtedly, they want to know what we do. Rarely do we ask, "Who are you?"

I remember a conversation I had with my line manager back in the days when my career was a central part of my life. She was having a hard time at work so had decided to hand in her notice. I was surprised because she was so dedicated and well respected. I tried to get her to stay, but she was adamant and said, "Anna, none of us are indispensable." At the time I thought it was a rather harsh comment; however, a few years later, when I was made redundant, I came to see just how true that statement is. I vowed back then to never invest my life in a job or anything career-related because, at any time, it can all come crushing down on you.

## Section summary

### In this section we have:

- Delved into how we arrived at our present state in our working and materialistic world.
- Examined some of the factors that have shaped our current identity.
- Seen that a lot of what has occurred in our lives has been beyond our influence.

I trust that you also recognise that nothing is set in stone and that you possess all the necessary tools to transform how you live the remainder of your life. All you need is a real desire to make it happen.

And if you really desire a better life, one that is based on your true values, then the next section will be your guide. It's the same method I used to change my life and it's the one I teach my clients. However, nothing ever happens unless you act. So, I encourage you to read each step and then, without hesitation, take action.

## PART THREE

## WHAT WILL YOU DO WITH THE REST OF YOUR LIFE?

*"What has been seen cannot be unseen, what has been learned cannot be unknown."*
– C. A. Wolfe

We started this journey with the question "How did I get here?" and then went on a quest to find the answer. You may now understand that much of your life has been out of your control, prescribed to you through social conditioning to make sure you fit in and do as you are expected to do.

The following seven stages will help you on your journey back to your authentic self:

1. FREEDOM
2. INTUITION
3. AWARENESS
4. FLOW
5. ACCEPTANCE
6. AGEING
7. SPIRITUALITY

# 1 – Freedom

*"Since we cannot change reality,
let us change the eyes which see reality."*
— Nikos Kazantzakis

As I discussed earlier, our desire for freedom dominates much of our life. We looked at Maslow's hierarchy of needs and saw that he placed freedom near the top of his model. Freedom, according to Maslow, is important if you are to reach your full potential.

But how can you be free if you do not understand what freedom really is?

In the previous chapters, we explored how we are trapped in our belief that freedom can be found through materialistic gain and that we spend so much of our life chasing things in the hope we will feel free. Maybe to an extent having money and certain luxuries make us feel free – however, not if we keep on wanting more, not if we don't know when enough is enough, because then we will never be happy.

The question we also need to consider is: does freedom rest only on the physical?

People like Viktor Frankl, a concentration camp survivor, and Nelson Mandela, who spent twenty-seven years in prison, show us that what is perhaps more important is our state of mind.

## Part Three: What Will You Do with the Rest of Your Life?

And this is what I want you to focus on here because, in reality, creating the conditions that will give you physical freedom cannot happen if your mind is caught up in limiting stories. Put simply, if you want to be free, you will need to let go of all those beliefs you have about what you can or cannot do, who you must be or must not be and what you are good at or not good at. You will need to remove all those layers that have kept you from being free to be yourself.

So how do you do that? Well, firstly you need to accept that you hold the key to your freedom. Until you can do that, nothing else will change.

Let me put this into context for you.

I had a friend, Jason, whom I met when I was going through my divorce. He was working at the first mindfulness retreat I ever attended. People would comment about how they thought he was a healer because he had such dark eyes that it felt like he could see deep into your soul. It was his sensitivity and empathic character that connected us as soon as we met, and our mutual love for reggae.

Over the years, we stayed friends, and he helped me through some of my worst moments. He also became my personal trainer. I remember once, when we were training together, he pushed me so hard that I started crying, like so much that my nose began to run like a baby! And as I tried to contain myself, knowing the tears were not tears of being overstretched physically but the release of all the pain I was going through in my life, I felt embarrassed.

He shouted at me: "Let it go, Anna," while we were standing in the middle of a busy-ish public park.

I replied, "I don't have a tissue."

He screamed back, "Wipe it on your clothes!"

What was significant about this was that I had to overcome two obstacles that day. One was my habit of not showing my emotions – something I learned as a young girl so I could protect myself from being hurt and let down. The other was to give myself permission to just wipe my darn snot and tears on my clothes. That was me beginning to let go of control. When you grow up in an environment where you do not always feel safe, always being in control becomes your default mode. So Jason taught me to let go a little and to accept the messiness of life.

But he taught me something else: the desire for freedom can be dangerous if you do not truly understand how to be free. Jason was a free spirit and he reminded me of who I used to be. However, despite all the spiritual awareness he seemed to have, he was stuck in the idea that to be free you must reject everything in mainstream society, and because of this he struggled financially. He also became consumed by the injustices in this world.

I understand how difficult it can be to live in this world and not become overwhelmed by all the inequity but what good are we to anyone if we allow ourselves to do that? If Nelson Mandela had become so overwhelmed with the cruelty and injustice that his people had to live with, he would never have changed history. And Emmeline Pankhurst would not have been able to lead a movement that led women to get the right to vote had she sat at home just moaning about the state of the world.

I'm not suggesting you go out there and create a movement, unless of course that's what you want to do, but I am suggesting you think carefully about what you believe freedom is.

Jason once told me that I was part of the system, the system that he hated so much, because I was a teacher. I tried to explain that we cannot beat the system by being outside of it; we can only do it by being so involved that we can make an impact… Anyway, this is a little off the point. My friend's view of the world kept him trapped, not least in his head. He eventually couldn't find any way out other than to take his own life.

Why is this significant here? Because if you focus on the external conditions to feel free, you may never be truly liberated. There may be times in your life when everything is perfect but then in a split second that can all fall apart. Isn't it better to focus on developing an inner freedom that is not easily disturbed by the less reliable outer conditions?

### Action:

The question you need to answer is: how much do you believe that freedom is possible?

- Use your workbook or get a piece of paper and a pen, pencil or even paintbrush!
- Draw, write or paint what freedom looks like for you.
- Spend some time thinking about what stories you tell yourself about your life.
- Now go back to what you've written, drawn or painted and ask yourself:
  - Is this me talking or my parents, partner, teacher or other significant person?
  - Look deeply. Try to identify patterns. Is this how it has always been?

When you feel you've done enough, put everything down and move on to the next task.

## 2 – Intuition

*"I have been a seeker and I still am,
but I stopped asking books and the stars.
I started listening to the teachings of my soul."*
– Rumi

How often do you go by your gut instinct? In this section, we will explore what intuition is and why learning to trust it more is key to being more in tune with what you genuinely want to do and who you want to be.

Your gut instinct can tell you when your relationship or job is not good for you. However, you've probably learned not to trust that voice that whispers to you, or maybe you rarely, if ever, hear it. But to break free from past habits and constantly being pulled along by what others say or what is expected from you, you need to reconnect with the voice you have probably ignored for far too long.

### What is intuition?

The *Cambridge Dictionary* defines intuition as "(knowledge from) an ability to understand or know something immediately based on your feelings rather than facts".

The idea that we let our feelings guide us rather than logical reasoning is why we struggle so much to follow our intuition. From a young age we are taught that our feelings are not good indicators to guide us in the right direction. In fact, we are explicitly told we must take control of our emotions and feelings.

Modern society has moved so far towards the conceptual and the things we can prove through science that anything else is often seen as fluffy or slightly crazy. And this is fed by our human ego, which believes that only what we can see and explain can possibly exist. Science has become our new God, in partnership with social media, celebrities and the press.

Evidence suggests that our intuition resides within the realm of the unconscious mind. In a 2011 interview, acclaimed author Malcom Gladwell was questioned about his perspective on intuition. In response, he expressed that "there is a tremendous amount of expertise in the unconscious mind. These aren't things we can necessarily describe, explain or map out."

He went on to explain that this expertise is a "steady accumulation of knowledge that lies below the surface and comes out in the form of intuition".

Intuition is this sense of knowing. There's no logical reason; you just know.

If you look at some of the most successful people, you will notice they often say they don't know exactly how they got to where they are, except that they followed their gut feeling. People like Oprah Winfrey and Sting have often attributed their success to following their instinct. And even Einstein is quoted as having said, "I believe in intuitions and inspirations. I sometimes feel I am right. I do not know that I am right."

This brings me back to something I discussed earlier in the book – our leaning towards science for all the answers. We've got to the point of making science our new God, and scientists the modern-day heroes. This is a fundamentally flawed perspective. I'd even go as far as to argue it is also rather dangerous. It's not that science is entirely problematic. We have undoubtedly made significant advancements through research. The issue lies in our tendency to forget that science isn't absolute truth; by its very nature, it remains a working hypothesis. Yet, we place excessive reliance on it, and that's where the danger lies.

We have come to rely on science so much that we have lost the ability to trust our natural intuition. It is the inflated human ego that believes that only what a human can prove can possibly exist. Just to add here: I'm not implying we should all go off and become religious fanatics, because religion isn't necessarily the answer either, especially in the institutional sense. But we would do well to remember what some of our wise ancestors knew many hundreds and thousands of years ago.

"What has all this got to do with intuition?" you might be asking. Well maybe if we weren't convinced that the answers were all "out there" or that we needed confirmation from some sort of expert, then perhaps we would feel more confident to listen to our gut feeling.

One more point I want you to consider is the notion of 'free will' and what that means. Dr Bruce Lipton explains that the conscious mind has the capacity to "override the subconscious mind's pre-programmed behaviours", which he states are the "foundation of free will". In other words, we are not making decisions or choices based on our own free will but on our pre-programmed behaviours. When you follow your gut feeling, you are accessing your subconscious mind, which means you are also closer to accessing your deepest truth.

**Action:**

This is a simple contemplation. Sit in your quiet, safe place. Close your eyes and think about these questions:

- How often do you listen to those voices that speak to you from the inside?
- Do you trust your intuition?

If you want, you can write down what comes up, or move on to the next step.

## 3 – Awareness

*"If, then, I were asked for the most important advice I could give, that which I considered to be the most useful to the men of our century, I should simply say: in the name of God, stop a moment, cease your work, look around you."*

– Leo Tolstoy,
*Essays, Letters and Miscellanies*

Before you can begin to remove the layers of learned behaviour, you have to raise your level of self-awareness. Now before you go off thinking I'm trying to promote some sort of flowery, spiritual practice, let me explain.

Awareness isn't something only the enlightened can develop, nor is it necessary for you to follow a specific religion. It is simply paying attention to your thoughts, actions and behaviours. And asking yourself some simple questions like "Do I really want to do this?" or, "Do I think I should do it?" Self-awareness enables you to really get to know yourself. You will start to see that very often you are doing things out of habit and sometimes you are just fulfilling the expectations of others.

There is another important outcome you can gain from going on this path to self-awareness, and that is getting to know the version of yourself that you have become so attached to that you don't dare change it. For example, I have this belief that I don't need anyone: "I'm so strong that I can handle everything on my own." And there is an element of truth in that. I am very self-sufficient but there is a part of that story that goes back to feeling I can't trust anyone. So when you start to observe your behaviours, you may become aware of how these thoughts you have of yourself keep you repeating patterns that are often harmful.

As your self-knowledge increases, you will notice how much more confident and empowered you feel. When you reconnect with who you truly are, beneath all the history and social conditioning, you will begin to feel almost invincible.

## What is awareness?

The *Oxford English Dictionary* defines awareness as "knowledge or perception of a situation or fact".

Sounds straightforward; however, our perception is not always the healthiest way to see things, because it is distorted by our past conditioning – something I've talked about at length already.

I like to define awareness as being fully conscious and mindful of who you are and what is happening by being present in the moment.

If you are currently going through a difficult time in your life, you might be thinking, *Of course I know what's going on right now. He/she cheated on me. I'm feeling angry.* Or maybe it's more like: *I'm devastated because my life is crumbling.* And to a certain extent, that is exactly what's going on right now. But is that all that's going on? What else might be playing out right now? Has a memory that lay dormant from your childhood been triggered?

To find out what is really happening for you in the present moment, you need to explore your inner world like you never have before. And to do that you need to raise your awareness.

Until you fully understand yourself, you are a victim of your past habits and your uncontrolled reactions. With this higher level of awareness comes freedom.

### The awareness model

Awareness is about taking full responsibility for your life. It's connecting with your inner self and exploring the places that you have avoided in the past. However, taking responsibility is not about blame. By taking responsibility, you can self-correct. If you accept blame, especially when it's not warranted, it's disabling and has a negative effect on you.

This diagram shows the process you will go through as you start to become aware. Self-awareness is about observing yourself. If you've ever met someone who seems to always be at peace, no matter what is going on, it's most likely because they have come to fully accept themselves. They don't spend too much time dwelling on the past or blaming themselves for mistakes.

## The Awareness Model

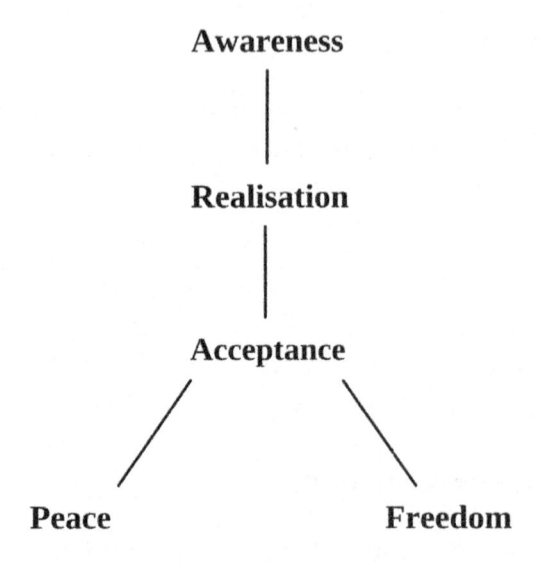

**Awareness**
|
**Realisation**
|
**Acceptance**
/          \
**Peace**        **Freedom**

In the first few weeks, and possibly months, after my marriage ended, my mind was nothing but crazy and out of control. One minute I was thinking about how to salvage my marriage, all the tricks I could play to just get things back to how they were, and the next I wanted my husband out of my life. I felt betrayed, angry and lost. There was a lifetime of stories attached to our marriage, as is expected when you've been with someone for so long, and it wasn't until I faced those stories that I was able to begin to break free from them. That's why it is so important that you turn inwards and be honest with yourself about the narratives you cling to as your reality.

For me, it was facing the truth about my relationship and how unhappy I really was. The whole partnership rested on me playing the role of the dependable and strong one. Just as I did when I was a child, staying in the background, not demanding too much and certainly not depending on others. And what this did was breed resentment that I never allowed to surface except when things became too much, and then it would be expressed as anger.

Had I known how much this habit of not asking for anything from anyone was affecting me and my relationships, then maybe I'd have made healthier life choices.

Until you recognise these patterns in your life, you are destined to keep playing them out.

Pema Chödrön advises that you **"go to the places that scare you"** because it is in those places that you will see clearly your greatest fears.

I want to return to the topic of mindfulness for a while because it is the practice that will help you learn how to pay attention to your thoughts and then also to your actions.

Perhaps this is the first time you've ever been asked to sit still with your thoughts, and so it might feel like an alien concept to you. And you may be under the impression that meditating will bring you to a calm place – that you will bliss out. That may happen at times; however, that is only the by-product. What you really want is to use your meditation to get to know your mind. So when you sit still, as recommended in the following action, instead of finding it peaceful, it's possible you'll have the opposite experience. And then you may think it's not working, but if you are brave enough to stick with it, you might begin to notice things about yourself you never did before.

I first started practising mindfulness meditation during my divorce. And each time I sat, I would end up crying, not because it was hard but because I stopped to listen to what was actually going on inside. I was angry, hurt and scared, but as long as I kept busy, I didn't give it too much attention. However, when I sat on that cushion and everything was silent, I had no choice but to pay attention. This is the part of mindfulness that people don't feel comfortable with, because it can bring up things we find difficult. And yet it is in those moments of unease that we make discoveries about ourselves that ordinarily we wouldn't.

For me, it was during those tears that I realised how much of myself I'd denied over the course of my life. It was in those moments that I was able to see how much of my past was still playing out in my present, determining who I was. And it wasn't easy to come to the realisation that not only did the people who were supposed to love me let me down, but the biggest struggle was accepting how much I'd let myself down. However, the beauty of sticking with the uncomfortable is that on the other side is clarity, which is what we ultimately want so we can live the rest of our life at peace with it all.

But I want to give you a word of warning: if you are going through a difficult time and find sitting in silence or even listening to a guided meditation isn't helpful, then don't do it. I also highly recommend that you speak to your doctor if you are struggling. It is important that you take care of yourself and do what is right for you at this moment.

**Action:**

I always recommend learning to incorporate some form of self-compassion practice. A simple one you can do wherever you are and at any time is as follows:

Stand with your feet firmly planted on the ground, preferably barefooted. It's even better if you can do this outside on the grass or even the beach! The idea is to be rooted in the earth or as close to it as you can, so indoors is fine too.

Close your eyes and breathe in through your nose, all the way from your belly, up through your chest, lungs and throat, and slowly release through your nose.

Let your body sink into the ground and feel your connection to the earth.

Imagine yourself being supported by the ground beneath you, holding you up, like a tree or mountain – solid and strong.

Keep the breath moving through your body. Let yourself be held by the earth, with your feet firmly rooted in the ground.

And if it helps, you might want to place a hand over your heart, repeat a few words that feel comfortable. Maybe something like "I am safe, I am well, I am happy…"

Do this for five or ten minutes, or more depending on how it works best for you. Then let go of the meditation and continue with your day. You can repeat this anytime you feel overwhelmed or just in need of some breathing space.

You can find additional resources on my website, annazannides.com.

## 4 – Flow

*"May what I do flow from me like a river, no forcing and no holding back, the way it is with children."*
— Rainer Maria Rilke

Have you noticed that when you do something you love, time seems to fly by, but when you do something you really don't enjoy, time seems to stop?

I remember when I was doing a job I found boring, I'd watch the clock from the minute the day started, and minutes felt like hours. I was literally counting my life down. However, when I am writing or with my family, walking in nature or exploring new places, there never seems to be enough time.

How can this be possible? After all, an hour is an hour whatever you are doing.

Well, it's because when we are doing what we love doing, we are in flow. But what does 'flow' mean?

Mihaly Csikszentmihalyi, a Hungarian psychologist, is well known for his work on happiness and the importance of flow. He famously said: "The best moments in our lives are not passive, receptive, relaxing times. The best moments usually occur if a person's body or mind is stretched to its limits in a voluntary effort to accomplish something difficult and worthwhile."

The idea of flow and its role in happiness isn't new nor completely attributed to the likes of Csikszentmihalyi. The Taoists talked about *Wu Wei*, which translates as 'the flow state'. This is when, instead of doing an act, one becomes it. Csikszentmihalyi explained it as being so involved in an activity that nothing else seems to matter. People enjoy the experience so much they will continue doing it, even if the cost is great, just for the sake of doing it.

It goes without saying that if being in a state of flow is what brings us joy, then surely we must find ways to be in that state more often. But in a world where we hardly have time to stop and think, it can seem there is no time for the things we enjoy. So what we do is find ways to distract ourselves from the boredom or dissatisfaction of life that do not give us the opportunity to be in a flow state. We live more and more in our unconscious state, rarely engaging with the subconscious mind, which is where, as I said before, our authenticity lives.

Let's look at flow from a different perspective. Bruce Lee once gave an interview where he said, "Empty your mind. Be formless, shapeless, like water. When you put water into a cup, it becomes the cup. Be like water."

He was trying to explain that happiness requires us to be flexible in body and mind. This flexibility allows us to stay open-minded and to not hold onto our views rigidly. With an open mind you are better able to change and adapt to the circumstances you meet in your daily life.

Let's take this a step further because I am sure you've experienced being in the flow at some point in your life. If you are an artist or work with your hands, you probably experience being in the flow often. But how does being in the flow play out in your day-to-day?

Releasing the desire to control life and craving certainty about the future are significant hurdles to overcome. While you can make plans and establish certain conditions, there is no assurance that things will go according to plan. Thus, it is beneficial to cultivate adaptability and a willingness to tolerate uncertainty and ambiguity.

In early 2020 I had decided to give up my job, sell my belongings and travel. The idea was I'd start in China and maybe do a bit of teaching there. Then I'd move on to Thailand, followed by Vietnam and take it as it came. After a long time battling with fear and the thought of having to leave my granddaughters, I left my job, sold my belongings and started packing the few things I wanted to hold onto. I had given notice on the apartment I was living in because I didn't want any restrictions on when to come back.

Then a virus in China was all over the news, so I thought it best to give China a miss and start my trip in Thailand. Over the following days, I sat in a rather empty flat, watching the world shut down. Nonetheless I was persistent, and I'd made some connections in Bali who reassured me they were safe. So I booked a one-way ticket to Bali with the intention of just waiting it out there while I wrote my book. I'd just gone downstairs to hand the keys of my car to the man who had bought it when my phone pinged with a message.

*Hey Anna, we've gone into lockdown too!*

It was from the lady in Bali who had assured me a few hours earlier that everything was fine. And there I was: no job, no car, no furniture and about to be homeless, again! I had a small pot of savings that I was going to use for my travels but it was always my intention to work while I was travelling, and it is much cheaper to live in Asia than the UK. I went into panic mode, like I'm sure many of us did when the world began to lock down. For days, all sorts of scenarios were going through my head, keeping me awake at night: *I'll be homeless, I'll have to go live with my kids, I'll run out of money soon.*

Then, one day, I stood still in the middle of the front room, put my hands up and shouted, "I surrender!"

It wasn't the first time in my life that things just fell apart and I should have known that plans never go exactly to plan. In that moment, when I gave up the struggle and decided to 'go with the flow', I felt a huge relief. Not only was it all out of my control but, just like me, there were millions of people across the world in the same position, or worse.

Strangely, once I surrendered control, things started to fall into place. The landlady had put the flat up for sale but because of the pandemic, selling was going to be a challenge, so she agreed I could stay. Luckily, I had my bed – I was going to give it away, so I was fortunate to have a roof over my head and a bed to sleep on.

Then I got speaking to a friend I hadn't heard from in a long time and happened to mention my situation. We had trained to teach together and he now worked in a school nearby. By the end of that day, I had a job. And I bought myself an old car with some of the money I was going to use for my travels.

It wasn't ideal but somehow it fell into place. Not only that but I felt lucky to not have been stranded in a strange country on my own, in the middle of a pandemic that I certainly never saw coming.

But what does this have to do with flow?

The point I'd like to leave you with here is that to be happier and more at peace with your life, you need to get comfortable living in flow – you need to feel at ease with not knowing what is around the corner, because you never really know. You can make assumptions; you can even make a wish but you have to learn to be okay even when things are not okay. And to do that you have to cultivate a sense of peace with things as they unfold. Learning to trust the process might not be easy but I can guarantee you that it is liberating.

Back in 2020, when my plans didn't go to plan, what I didn't know was that it was for the best. It seemed, once again, that the universe had my back.

Eventually I left the job I took on to get me through the pandemic. I set up my own business and bought my own home. I moved out of London to a quieter, more peaceful place and, best of all, I didn't leave my children and grandchildren. But, more importantly, I realised that my desire to travel was really hiding the fact that I was bored and disappointed with my life. I was looking for a thrill and a distraction from my own life. Being forced to sit down and stop made me see that the answer wasn't in running away but in staying put so I could create the life I wanted, right here.

**Action:**

Now it's over to you – time for you to reflect on your relationship with control and flow. Using a notebook, or in the downloadable workbook, write down how you relate to what we covered above.

On a scale of 1 to 10 (1 being not at all and 10 being completely comfortable), how do you feel about living in flow and not needing to know what's around the corner?

And how does this affect your day-to-day life?

## 5 – Acceptance

*"True belonging only happens when we present
our authentic, imperfect selves to the world,
our sense of belonging can never be greater than
our level of self-acceptance."*
– Brené Brown

People often associate acceptance with weakness or surrendering and giving up.

That is why when I introduce the idea of acceptance when working with people who are going through a difficulty such as divorce, their first reaction can be defensive. They may say something like "I can't accept that he treated me so badly" or "I won't accept that she cheated on me."

So to reassure you, I'm not talking about accepting being treated badly and acceptance isn't about taking responsibility for the bad behaviour of others.

The *Oxford English Dictionary* defines acceptance as "the action of consenting to receive something offered". The words 'welcoming' and 'embracing' are synonyms of acceptance. So if we come from that perspective, the idea that we might have been consenting or welcoming a person to cheat on us or treat us badly is enough to make anyone angry and reject the idea of acceptance.

Anger is a natural response to being hurt. I remember when I was going through my divorce that sometimes my anger would just take over and if anyone had suggested I forgive my ex-husband, I don't even want to imagine my response.

Acceptance isn't about you denying your pain or putting up with anyone or anything that is harmful to your well-being. You don't accept the other person to let them off the hook; you work on acceptance to free yourself.

Acceptance is about saying "It's happened!" "Yes, they let me down" "Yes, my relationship isn't what I thought it was" "Yes, they cheated on me" and whatever else may be your story. This enables you to begin the process of letting go.

If you can't change it and you can't mend it, then what choice do you have but to accept it?

So, acceptance is a sort of coming to terms, letting it be and finding some peace with whatever has happened. It's when you decide to give up fighting and start to move forward in your life.

## The different aspects of acceptance

After my divorce I struggled to come to terms with the lost dreams and, perhaps more importantly, the realisation that I'd allowed myself to lose myself in my relationship. We've talked about this earlier in the book but I want to return to it here because without self-forgiveness you will not be able to create that life you so desperately want. If you are still holding on to self-critical thoughts about the 'should haves' and 'could haves', you will be holding yourself back. You must come to terms with your past and find a way to leave it where it belongs.

And perhaps this one is just as difficult: accepting that you are not perfect, and you never will be. Perhaps you too have hurt others or let them down. Do you have the courage to look at that possibility?

This isn't a call for you to start blaming yourself; it is, however, a prompt to get you to take responsibility. It is a hard task to look at one's life through a non-judgemental lens, to own up to the times when you may have not been so nice to someone. But when you've been honest about your own less virtuous actions, you can release the guilt and shame you might be holding onto.

When I look back at my life, I find it hard to accept there were times in my marriage when I didn't want to be in it but would never have ended it had my ex-husband not given me the excuse. I am sure I wasn't always nice to him or present with my children, because there was a part of me that wanted to be free from all that responsibility.

In her book *Prime Time*, Jane Fonda asks her readers to do a 'life review' and suggests that to do that you must first look back. You may be thinking this contradicts what you've read earlier, especially in regard to acceptance. However, you cannot go forward without letting go of your past. And to let go of the things that play on your mind, you must first be completely honest with yourself about your role in it all.

## Time is a healer

Contrary to what we are often told, time on its own is never a healer. Unfortunately, in my line of work, I see it all too often – people who live in the past, stuck in an event that happened once upon a time and those who identify themselves so closely with a situation that however much time goes by, they never really move on from it.

Why do people do that? Because the alternative is to let that story go and move past it, but if you are so close to it, you may believe that it is who you are. One thing I did to change the narrative I was holding onto about being divorced was to stop calling myself 'divorced' and I started saying, "I'm single." I even stopped writing 'divorced' on official forms and replaced it with 'single', not because I thought it was stigmatised but because I believe it to be irrelevant. In fact, our marital status should not be of any relevance in the workplace, or anywhere else for that matter. It's simple shifts in how we perceive a past situation or ourselves that help us move on and, yes, this takes time but it also requires conscious effort.

Reflecting on your life might bring up some difficult emotions, so you should do it with a lot of self-compassion.

## What is self-compassion?

We live in a society that teaches us that putting ourselves first is selfish, that somehow we deserve our own attention less than others do. Often in our relationships, we give so much that we forget what it's like to ask for what we want – if we even know what we want – and then after years of self-neglect we start to resent our partner or others in our life. What we are rarely taught is that it is our duty to put ourselves first.

Putting yourself first does not mean you don't think about others or that you become self-centred. It means you learn to listen to what you want and need so that you are better placed to be there for yourself and others.

As I already covered in the previous pages, self-compassion requires you to fully accept yourself, past and present. It means you accept your imperfections and stop striving for perfection, which is an impossible ideal. And you give yourself the same level of respect that you give others, or perhaps even more.

If you've not taken care of yourself before, now is the time to start. If that feels alien to you or selfish, then you have a lot of work to do because real change starts by accepting that you are worthy. Self-care can be small, such as taking a long bath without disruption, or big, like ending a toxic relationship or walking away from a job that is making you unhappy.

When I work with individuals or groups, I find the part most people struggle with is self-kindness. Most of us are familiar with the self-critic and you may find it quite natural to step into the harsh self-critical thoughts – being kind to yourself isn't always an easy habit to cultivate. Changing how you relate to yourself requires resolve and commitment.

Becoming your own best friend changes every aspect of your life. There is nothing more empowering than knowing yourself. But when you also reach a place of full self-acceptance, you become invincible. When you know yourself, other people have less power over you and they can't make you feel bad about yourself when they judge you based on their own views. If you have the courage to dig deep to reach a level of total self-respect, then you can be fearless in your life.

One of the most difficult things you can do is accept that the people who hurt you or let you down did so not because of you but because of their own shortcomings. If you are brave enough, this is when you look at their actions, knowing they did the best they could with the tools they had. And here's the game changer: if you really love who you are, then how can you resent any of your past? Isn't that why you are the amazing person you are today?

I know it's hard to offer that sort of compassion towards someone who has caused you to suffer; however, I find it the most liberating way to view my past. You see, when you are at peace with who you are at your core, you look back with a sense of gratitude, because it is our darkness that helps us grow. Otherwise, if you hold on to resentment and anger, you continue to accept those people into your life.

The hardest thing you can do is to live knowing the person who hurt you or let you down may never apologise or, worse, even blame you. Coming to terms with the years lost with someone that was never worthy of your time or accepting that your parents didn't give you what you needed is your life's work. But when you finally get to that place, you are free.

**Reflections and actions**

In the following few paragraphs, you will find simple ways to bring self-compassion into your life.

Although I can't go into as much depth or detail here as I do with my 1:1 clients, or in my courses, the following list is a great place to start.

1. **Change the narrative by paying attention to it.**

    This is where awareness comes in. When you begin to consciously and purposefully start to pay attention to that inner voice, you will notice the familiar conversations. You'll need to go back to the reflection on page 164 to refresh your memory on what your habitual thoughts are.

What patterns have you noticed, if any? Those repeating thoughts are your inner narrative and if they do not serve you well, then they are what needs to change.

2. **Make time for self-care.**

   One of the practices I teach in mindfulness is to get people to look at how much of their time they spend doing things that deplete their energy as opposed to things that nourish them.

   A nourishing activity might be going to bed early or taking a hot shower slowly rather than in a rush. Depleting activities could be your daily commute and after-work meetings.

   Keep a log for a few days so you can write down all the activities you do that make you feel better and the ones that drain your energy. Once you have identified these, consider what you can change.

3. **Kill the self-critic!**

   The best way to work with the self-critic is to develop the capacity to recognise it before it takes over your train of thought.

   Pioneering research psychologist Kristin Neff concluded that there are three components to self-compassion.

One is to become mindful of your thoughts and feelings by being present for them, rather than getting lost in them as we would normally.

Once we have noticed these habitual thoughts, we can acknowledge the fact that all humans have these painful experiences. And we accept that they are all part of being human – there is nothing wrong with us.

With that insight and recognition, we can respond with kindness rather than thinking we have failed.

Clinical psychologist Chris Germer offers the following ways to be more self-compassionate:

Develop the capacity to ask yourself: "What do I need?" Germer elaborates that when someone else asks us "What do you need?" it touches our heart but we don't usually ask ourselves that question. He also adds that we can go further by ensuring that when we ask ourselves "What do I need?", we do it with kindness.

The next thing Germer recommends is physical touch. He explains that when things go wrong, we find it comforting to be held or touched by another person in a loving and caring way. He adds that research

> suggests we can put our hands on our heart or on another soothing place "in a way that does shift our physiology from a threat state to a care state, especially when we are doing it as an act of kindness".
>
> This act of self-compassion is one of the core mindfulness practices I teach. It is an invitation to put your two hands over your heart and allow them to linger there for a while, feeling the warmth of your hands. And just see what happens.

Before we move on to the next section, I'd like to invite you to make a promise to yourself that every day you will do something kind for yourself.

## 6 – Ageing

*"Most people don't grow up. Most people age. They find parking spaces, honor their credit cards, get married, have children, and call that maturity. What that is, is aging."*
– Maya Angelou

The traditional approach to addressing ageing within society is no longer effective, as we are now experiencing longer lifespans and the existing frameworks are just not fit for purpose anymore.

As previously discussed, in the past, life was characterised by a more linear trajectory that included lifelong careers and relationships, and retirement typically occurred around the age of sixty, which was close to the average life expectancy at the time.

Today the average life expectancy is around eighty and it is likely to increase to well into the nineties in the future. You would think that having an additional decade of life would make us ecstatic, but it seems that with this extra time has come some problems.

'Grey divorce' is a term that first started being used in the US in 2004 following research showing that although the general divorce rate was in decline, for those over fifty it was on the rise. Studies found several reasons for this increase, including infidelity, growing apart, financial management and addictions.

Due to longer lifespans and higher divorce rates, an increasing number of elderly individuals are experiencing living alone. This is compounded by the loss of social connections that often occurs after retirement. As a result, loneliness among seniors has become a significant issue, highlighting the need to consider ways to make later life more fulfilling.

Numerous studies have highlighted various factors that contribute to a long and healthy life. Some of the most significant factors include genetics, lifestyle choices, social connections, stress management and access to healthcare. Genetics may play a role in determining lifespan, but lifestyle choices such as regular exercise, a balanced diet and avoiding harmful habits like smoking and excessive drinking are also crucial.

In addition to these factors, other elements such as maintaining a positive outlook, engaging in meaningful activities and pursuing lifelong learning have also been linked to longevity.

I would like to include additional factors that you should take into account as you get older.

- Your attitude towards ageing is crucial in maintaining a positive outlook as you age. It is not about distracting yourself from the inevitability of death, but rather being grateful for every moment of life and making the most of the time you have left. And it is pointless to waste time on regret.

- Ageing should be seen as a gift, a time to make things right, to have important conversations and to express what needs to be said.
- Keeping your sense of curiosity alive and remaining open to new experiences and learning can protect your mind from becoming stagnant and disinterested in life.

Upon reaching the age of fifty, I experienced a feeling of panic as I realised that the years already lived were likely greater in number than those still to come. Reflecting on this, I couldn't help but feel that the first fifty years of my life had passed by in a blur, with many moments when I wasn't fully present. Interestingly, after my divorce, I didn't struggle with feelings of betrayal or disappointment towards my ex-husband; instead, I had difficulty coming to terms with the passage of time and the realisation that life is fleeting.

On the day I was deciding whether to salvage my marriage or let it go, I went out into the garden with a blanket, despite the late hour and chilly weather. Sitting there for hours, I wept and attempted to logically reason whether or not to release myself from those thirty years of life. It was then that I had a startling realisation: I had been using my marriage as a crutch to hold myself back. Though I longed to explore the world and write a book, I would always dismiss these dreams with excuses like "I don't have the time" or "My needs aren't important." If I were to end my marriage, what excuse would I have left? The fear of losing excuses transformed into a sense of liberation, as I realised that, without excuses,

I could become anyone I desired. With determination, I extinguished my cigarette and wiped my tears, resolving to tell him to leave in the morning. I refused to compromise my life any further.

Later that year, during my visit to Nepal, I stepped outside the guest house's small dining room to smoke a cigarette and met Lez. He was unlike any man I had encountered before, a spiritual figure who some might call a shaman. As we stood together, gazing at the garden, he posed a question that left me confused and even a bit angry: "Have you forgiven yourself yet?" Lez didn't offer any further explanation, but his question lingered with me over the next few days until I finally delved deeper into its meaning. I realised that I was having a hard time forgiving myself for not staying true to my authentic self, and instead living a life that met everyone else's expectations. This realisation was heart breaking because it had been deeply ingrained in me for so long. Achieving forgiveness in this area of my life would require a lot of hard work.

It dawned on me that in order to stay authentic and true to ourselves, we must always bear in mind that life is finite and too precious to be lived as if we have an eternity. As I grappled with my struggle to forgive myself, I realised that my anger wasn't solely directed towards me, but also towards society for deceiving me with false beliefs as a child that made me veer away from my genuine self.

My work with individuals living with cancer brought me face to face with the realities of death and dying, and it was during this time that I realised the true value of life. My Buddhist teachers, who spoke about the concept of impermanence, helped me appreciate that life is too precious to squander on trivial pursuits. As I watched people with the same look of fear in their eyes join the group, I realised that receiving a cancer diagnosis changes everything for an individual. It's unfortunate that we need such reminders to recognise the sacredness of life.

Once I facilitated a support group for individuals suffering from incurable cancer, which included two elderly members who faced unique challenges. One of the members was not only battling cancer but also had to cope with the recent loss of her husband. Whenever we interacted, she appeared to have lost her reason to live. The other member, an eighty-year-old man who appeared scruffy, warned me during our initial meeting that he had Tourette's and might unintentionally shout out some profanities. He felt compelled to apologise in advance. However, I assured him that, having grown up in Tottenham, I had probably heard it all before.

In the following weeks, both individuals opened up and shared their tales of regret. The man, in particular, confided in us that his children didn't like him and were unwilling to communicate with him due to his past behaviour towards them.

So, I asked both of them this question: "How would you like to be remembered? As miserable, unloving, individuals, or happy, loving parents?"

A few weeks later as I walked into the cancer support centre the lady's daughter was sitting in the waiting room. She introduced herself to me and told me how much her mother had changed. She had started going swimming and smiled a lot more. In that session the man told us that he had apologised to his children, and they had started to visit him again.

The question of "How do you want to be remembered?" is perhaps the most important way to make ageing and later life more meaningful. It is in those later years that you can use the wisdom you have gained to give back and to leave behind something that will benefit others, in whatever way you can.

However, many reach their older years and begin to live in fear. Fear of what? I wonder. If it's death, then what is the point fearing the inevitable? It seems such a waste of life. Perhaps a more useful attitude to have is that, now more than ever, life is precious.

**Action:**

Now I'd like to ask you the same question I asked the two people in my group: "How would you like to be remembered?"

You might be thinking, *But I'm only young, I don't need to think about that right now.* Well, if you are young, then keeping this question at the forefront of your mind will serve you well and it will keep reminding you that life is too short to squander it being unhappy.

## 7 – Spirituality

*"If you find no one to support you on the spiritual path, walk alone."*
– The Buddha

As we near the end of our journey together, I would like to address the topic of spirituality. In a world that has become more focused on materialism and reliant on scientific evidence, the notion there may be more to life than what we can physically observe is often dismissed as outdated or primitive.

Spirituality is a broad term that can mean different things to different people, but it generally refers to an individual's personal beliefs and practices related to their understanding of the non-physical aspects of life. Spirituality can involve a connection to a higher power, such as a God or universal energy, as well as beliefs about the nature of the soul, consciousness and the afterlife. It may also involve practices such as meditation, prayer and other forms of reflection or self-exploration aimed at fostering a deeper understanding of oneself and one's place in the world.

Spirituality has been co-opted by some New Age leaders who have commercialised it, turning it into a product to be marketed and sold. Unfortunately, this has resulted in turning spirituality into something that may seem unappealing or even disingenuous to those who do not subscribe to this approach. However, it is important to recognise that this commercialisation is not representative of spirituality as a whole and there are still genuine and meaningful ways to explore one's spirituality without falling into the trappings of consumerism. Ultimately, it is up to each individual to find their own path and means of exploring spirituality that resonate with them personally.

The essence of spirituality lies in attributing meaning and purpose to our lives, rather than inflating our ego or claiming an elevated position. Engaging in spiritual materialism is a misguided approach. Instead, spirituality involves comprehending our place in the world and the interconnectedness of all things and approaching life with wonder and amazement. When we recognise that our life is not solely about self-gratification but also about giving and leaving a positive legacy, our existence becomes more profound. It is not relevant which religion one belongs to or whether one is an atheist; what matters is exhibiting love and compassion towards all living beings, living a purposeful life and cherishing every day we have.

That is the true meaning of spirituality.

**Action:**

Your last task is to reflect on your spiritual beliefs and practices. Do you have a deep spiritual life, or do you believe it is unnecessary?

Remembering what I covered earlier on about Maslow, it might be useful for you to think about how you can improve the quality of your life so you can reach your full potential. And to do that you may want to consider your place in the universe, rather than limiting yourself to just this small world you can see in front of you.

I'm not suggesting you become religious if you are not, because religion and spirituality are not the same thing. It's more about realising the profound privilege of human life and how important you are in the grand scheme of things.

So take some time to really contemplate your spirituality and what that might mean to you.

## Closing Note

The progress of the world is dependent on an individual's personal growth because we are the result and part of the entire human existence. For self-improvement to happen, it is crucial to develop self-awareness. Without fully understanding your own being, there can be no foundation for proper thinking, and if you don't know yourself, then change is unattainable.

It is possible that you are content with following the rules and norms of this world and you might even agree that they are desirable and appropriate because they are taking you in the direction you want to go. However, it is crucial you assess whether the world you participate in aligns with your values and beliefs. If it does not, you may need to seek change or alternative systems that are a better fit with your worldview. Ultimately, it is up to you to determine the kind of world you want to live in.

In the past, particularly for White males, it may have been simpler to have confidence in the idea that they were living in a just and fair world, and that the world was progressing in the right direction.

As time has passed, it has become increasingly difficult to maintain the belief that we are living in an ideal world, and adjusting to this world has become more challenging.

The state of being intoxicated, struggling with addiction and wasting countless hours on social media are not problems that need to be overcome solely for the sake of becoming better members of society. Rather, they are symptomatic of a deeper issue: a lack of fulfilment in our lives. If you were truly invested in a meaningful existence, these problems would not have a hold on you. When you lack a clear direction and sense of purpose, you become lost and are more likely to seek out distractions to fill the void.

You may sometimes adopt false objectives, such as pursuing more money or other things that are not actually what you truly desire. These tendencies – such as greed, materialism, addiction and self-sabotage – are not the root problem, but rather symptoms of a larger issue. It's not a reflection of personal inadequacy; it's a flaw in the underlying system or programme. This is why you may feel compelled to disengage from it, leading to feelings of depression and a desire to withdraw. Despite being told that everything is okay and that medication can solve the problem, it's not a matter of physical illness but rather a rebellion of the soul.

It may not be apparent that there are other options besides medication to help you keep moving forward. Because this is such a contentious issue, it can be challenging to argue for alternatives, especially when many individuals credit medication with saving their life. It's not my place to judge whether medication is right or wrong, or whether it is inherently good or bad. The purpose of medication is to enable people to function in the world they are presented with, which creates a catch-22 situation: how can you escape that world? What alternatives are available besides just coping and adjusting to it? Although I cannot provide a definitive solution, your desire to escape and your inquiry about how to do so will ultimately lead to your liberation.

Loneliness, disconnection and the feeling of emptiness can all be improved when you step into your authenticity and when you realise the preciousness of your human life. And when you align your thinking with your feelings, you will find a deeper sense of peace.

I urge you to move away from living from your mind and direct more attention to living from your heart. To follow your gut feelings, let go of control a little and live more in the flow of life.

Before I go, I want to wish you the courage to embrace your true self, and if you are uncertain of who that person is, I hope that I have given you enough to start that journey back to your authentic self.

And – as in the words of Rumi, "I have been a seeker and I still am, but I stopped asking books and the stars. I started listening to the teachings of my soul" – never stop being a seeker.

# Resources and Additional Support

You can download the workbook from my website, annazannides.com/how-did-i-get-here.

This resource complements the tasks and reflections in *How Did I Get Here?* And provides invaluable support. By sharing your name and email address, you'll gain access to weekly emails full of inspiration and life advice directly from Anna.

Your journey doesn't have to end here. Visit annazannides.com to explore a variety of self-paced programmes, downloadable resources and workshops thoughtfully designed to enhance the teachings in this book.

However, if you want further support to implement any of what you have read, then working with Anna on a 1:1 basis may be what you need. You can find out about Anna's coaching programmes and other ways to work with her at annazannides.com/workwithme.

If you have a question or want further advice, you can email Anna at anna@annazannides.com.

> *"Anna's honest, gentle, down-to-earth and compassionate approach was just what I needed. Anna has a wonderful gift."*
> – Betty, cancer survivor

## Book Anna to Speak

Book Anna to speak at your event or to run a workshop to inspire, entertain and deliver a truly life-changing experience for everyone in attendance.

With Anna's profound understanding of mindfulness, coaching and Buddhism, you can be confident your event will be a breath of fresh air!

To find out more about booking an event with Anna, visit annazannides.com/hireme.

> *"I would like to say thank you with all my heart for taking the time to share your wisdom. You always hit it on the nail for me personally."*
> – Helen, coaching client

## About the Author

Anna Zannides is living proof that every single one of us has the capability to overcome our adversity and create the most extraordinary life we can imagine, if only we have the courage to listen to what's authentically calling us.

Even though Anna grew up around addiction and dysfunction, she didn't let her past experiences and lack of formal qualifications hold her back. Later in life, Anna achieved a first-class honours degree and built a successful career in education. However, after going through a divorce and redundancy, Anna knew it was time for change. She made a conscious decision to break free from the lifestyle that had been a constant source of conflict in her life.

That's when Anna found solace in Buddhism and decided to train as a mindfulness teacher with the Mindfulness Association and renowned teachers such as Rob Nairns and Trish Bartley. She later studied coaching and NLP, successfully gaining accreditation as a personal coach.

Now she has the privilege of working with people who are going through life challenges such as cancer, loss and relationship endings. It's Anna's way of giving back and helping others navigate through difficult times, drawing from her own experiences.

Anna has been featured in several publications, including *Saga Magazine* and *Let's Mend*. She has also appeared on many podcasts, sharing her insights on how we lose sight of our innermost potential, leaving us unaware of our authentic self.

Anna lives a contemplative life. She devotes her time to writing, travelling, running her business, nurturing her relationships with family and friends and embracing her Buddhist practice.

## Connect with Anna

Instagram: @annazannides
Facebook: www.facebook.com/AnnaZannidesAuthor
LinkedIn: www.linkedin.com/in/annazannides

Printed in Great Britain
by Amazon